Beginning the Rest of Your Life

GUIDE TO AN ACTIVE RETIREMENT

Harry Disston

ARLINGTON HOUSE PUBLISHERS
333 POST ROAD WEST
WESTPORT, CONNECTICUT 06880

Robert F. Dame, Inc.
1905 Huguenot Road
Richmond, Virginia 23235

Arlington House Publishers, Inc.
333 Post Road West
Westport, Connecticut 06880

Library of Congress Cataloging in Publication Data

Disston, Harry, 1899—
    Beginning the rest of your life.

    Includes index.
    1. Retirement. 2. Old age. I. Title.
HQ1062.D56   301.43'5   78-75301
ISBN 0-87000-518-9

Dedicated to

KATIE

*who provides the charm, grace, color,
and chief companionship in my active
"retirement" and says—with little
conviction—that I do too much, that
I am supposed to have retired and should
slow down, knowing full well that I will
not.*

Contents

Preface

This book is about retirement—or, more properly, about *not* retiring. It is also about growing older without growing old. Positively, it is about enjoying a useful and full life in one's later years. It is about wearing out rather than rusting out.

Hopefully, this book will appeal to, or at least interest, those already retired and those about to retire—a sizeable group, estimated to be about 25 million in 1980, around 11 percent of the population at that time. It might also be useful to those exceptional youngsters who, although it is far off, are sufficiently farsighted to plan now for their eventual retirement, and to those assisting and guiding others in this area.

The problems of retirement stem largely from its two basic characteristics. First, there is, on the one hand, no *compulsion* to be gainfully employed and, on the other, great difficulty in finding gainful employment if one wants or needs it. Second is inability, or great difficulty, to adjust to a fundamental change in life style. Herein we suggest means of dealing with these problems.

Retirement as a situation, a condition, a problem, has not always been with us. In days gone by, in the United States, the work force was composed almost wholly of men. Women maintained the home and reared the numerous children who were then an economic asset. The human life span was markedly shorter. Consequently, with few exceptions and excluding the wealthy, men worked at their occupations until they died.

In contrast, people today live longer and are healthier, and each year there is in increasing number of retired people. Largely because of mandatory retirement requirements at a specified age (now under attack), the tax structure, and liberal retirement pay benefits men and women are leaving their occupations, "retiring," with many years of living ahead of them—and are doing so at a progressively younger age. The lack of salary incentives for continued employment (again due to the tax structure) and the rising cost of "going to work" also contribute to early retirement.

Most, however, retire, or are required to, at age sixty-five, or between sixty and sixty-five. The characteristics and problems of retirement and aging are therefore related and similar. In this book "aging" and "the elderly" may well be substituted for "retirement" and "the retired."

Our society—government, politics, business, the mass news media, and even the younger members of the community—is becoming increasingly concerned with retirees and the aged senior citizens.

We hear a good deal about "senior citizens"; there is a growing number of retired persons' clubs and associations; the Army publishes a periodical especially for its retirees, and conducts annual conferences on a "second career" for its retired and retiring personnel; a large amount of advertising—real estate, investment, employment, vacation spots, and cruises—is slanted especially towards retired people.

This concern, throughout, is directed largely toward helping them, looking after them, providing for them; the seniors are viewed and treated in general as needy and incompetent, as people to be pitied and entertained. There are, of course, many retired and elderly who need aid and care and compassion, those who are able to do little for themselves. But so do many of all ages.

Here, however, we suggest retiring and aging in such a way that care and aid are *not* desired or necessary.

Most large business and industrial firms support a variety of activities which prepare their employees for retirement. These efforts are directed largely toward encouraging hobbies, developing skills in the management of small business, presenting opportunities for social and civic service, and toward a general promotion of "outside" interests.

The theme of this book is that one should not actually "retire," but rather that he or she continue to lead a full, useful, and purposeful life. Since the essence of living is physical and mental activity and continual growth, the retiree must exert special effort to maintain physical fitness and mental alertness, remain active, develop a useful purpose, continue a broad acquaintance and social activity, look ahead, and adopt a new, creative, active, and challenging life style.

In brief, the thrust of this work is that it is far better to wear out than to rust out.

Means of achieving that objective are herein set forth in reasonable detail.

For obvious and understandable reasons this book is addressed to men. Furthermore, retirement situations and problems (and their management) and concerns over retirement are much more relevant to men than they are to women.

Women, despite their "liberation" and their entry into both the labor and management fields in large proportions, are still primarily involved with maintaining a home, bearing and raising children, and having a man contribute the greater portion of the family income. In addition, women expect their men to provide for both of them in retirement and old age. Living satisfactorily in retirement is still basically and largely a male responsibility.

To the extent my experience and my observations permit, which is not much, I have extended the coverage of my comments here and there to include women. I am fully aware that these comments may be inadequate; but, necessarily, so be it.

My competence to address the subject convincingly is set forth in the introduction, "To Prove the Point."

Acknowledgments

While a number of people, directly and indirectly and sometimes unknowingly, assisted in the preparation of this book, I want especially to acknowledge the substantial assistance provided by Dr. John B. Lange, Dr. John F. McGavock and Dr. White McK. Wallenborn in reviewing the chapter "Keeping Physically Fit" and other portions of the typescript relating to medical matters, and for their helpful suggestions. I am grateful to Kay Williamson for her careful and intelligent typing of the manuscript and for some research. My wife, Katie, once again made wise and useful suggestions for improvement after reading the entire typescript.

To Prove the Point

I retired from a position of some responsibility with a large corporation in New York City five years before the mandatory retirement age. I moved to an abandoned farm some 300 miles away in Virginia and began to rehabilitate it for breeding, training, and boarding horses.

Currently, I operate my horse farm, attend to my active business as associate with a rapidly growing and prospering leasing company, work on my weekly newspaper column, magazine articles, and another book, and keep an eye on the small rural land company of which I am president.

A certain amount of time is devoted also to the nine civic, church, and military organizations of which I am president (six of them) or a director. I am a recorded judge, technical delegate, and steward of the American Horse Shows Association. (Thus far, I have passed the required biannual physical test.)

Each day, with few exceptions, I ride at least an hour and walk a brisk mile; about four times a week, except during the winter, I play tennis; and in the summer, additionally, I swim as often as I can. My weight is steadily one pound over what it was when I was graduated from college, and my pulse and blood pressure is little different from what it was at that time.

Since retiring, I also served as: Placement Director at the University of Virginia's Graduate School of Business Administration and headed its Development Committee; Director of School Relations for the Jefferson Professional Institute; Finance Chairman of the Republican Party of Virginia and Chairman of the Louisa County Republican Committee; a director of the local chapter of the American National Red Cross and the English Speaking Union. I have had published six books on horses, an article in the *Encyclopaedia Britannica*, and several magazine articles on equine, business, and military subjects.

I plan no expansion of my present activities—nor do I plan to curtail them, unless, of course, an organization of which I am a member asks me to do so. In due course I shall wear out. But for the foreseeable future I have no time to dwell on that eventuality.

The foregoing may appear to be immodestly boastful. It is not intended to be. It is stated only to demonstrate that I am practicing what I preach!

Beginning
the Rest of Your Life

1 *The Retirement Syndrome*

Most of us are so wrapped up in our jobs—through necessity and often also through enjoyment—that we have, or take, little time to reflect on our eventual retirement. Certainly we give little, if any, time or thought to planning for it, except in a routine sort of way. It is axiomatic that the busier we are in pursuit of our gainful occupations, the less we prepare for retirement. We know that we will have to face it one day, but we sweep it under the rug. Actually the busy ones are the ones who should be most concerned about retirement because they are least prepared for it.

Let's look at the situation: one day John and his wife Mary and Mr. General Manager and Mr. Staff Coordinator become aware (most often painfully) that this is the day he is to retire! Last month, last week, and yesterday—despite the retirement parties, cards, letters, gifts, and personal and telephoned good wishes—he was on the payroll, an active member of the organization. Now, one day later than yesterday, he is not. He is retired—complete with pension, gifts, a memory book, and good wishes.

"What are you going to do?" inquires the personnel vice president as he greets him in the reception line.

"Well, I'm not sure—going to look around, pay more attention to the garden, spend more time with the grandchildren, travel, and just take it easy."

In about two years, although he is now quite healthy, chances are good he will be dead. The cause? Boredom.

During the first several weeks of retirement, everything is hunky-dory. John sleeps in (and so does his wife for a change);

breakfast is leisurely, followed by a thorough perusal of the newspaper and a viewing of their favorite morning TV program. John feels superior and pleased with himself as his neighbors hurry to the train and bus carrying bulging briefcases. "Those poor guys who have to awaken to an early ringing of the alarm clock and ride that long distance to the office. Poor guys! Am I glad I don't have to!"

After about six weeks spent in leisurely bliss, taking it easy, loafing, the new-found inactivity palls a little. John gets restless and fidgety; strangely, he misses not having to shave in the morning and select the shirt and tie he will wear that day. Mary doesn't like the new experience of having John around the house all day; he interferes, rather than helps, when he accompanies her to the supermarket.

One day, about two months after his retirement, John decides to go to the office and call on some of his old friends. All of them greet him heartily, inquire about his retirement activities, health, and family, and express envy of his easy life. He is thus encouraged to make more and, unwittingly, longer visits. However, after several such visits to the office he begins to realize, reluctantly, that while his former associates are polite and demonstrate an interest in his well being, their attention seems to wander to the business at hand and that occasionally they seem a little hurried; he senses that he is intruding on a busy day, that he is diverting attention from serious matters and that his hosts will be glad when he is gone so that they can get back to work. John begins to feel just a little sorry for himself—unappreciated.

The pace decreases and creeping stagnation begins—John sleeps still a little later, spends more time before the TV tube, reads two morning and an evening paper, accompanies Mary on all of her shopping trips, reads fully all of the junk mail, plays a little bridge and some golf. He goes to the movies often and he and Mary "eat out" more than they used to when he was active with the company.

John tells Mary that he isn't feeling just right and seems to develop a number of minor ailments. With increasing frequency he is heard to say, "Oh, no, I'm too old for that."

As time drags on, John eats more and more and exercises less and less. He reads, listens and views more and participates in community and church activities less. His doctor tells John that he is much too overweight and that he should walk two miles each day, quit smoking, eat smaller better-balanced meals, and drink more water. The doctor suggests that John also participate in some community activity. Does John follow his doctor's advice? For a little while, reluctantly, yes; then not at all.

Two years and two weeks after his retirement—at which time he was healthy, vigorous, and interested—John dies.

Why? The cause? Bordeom. John was literally bored to death. He had nothing to do, no challenges, no obstacles, no problems, no objectives. John's life during the short period after his retirement was all intake and no output. He was of no use on this earth, so the Lord took him from it.

2   *An Alternative*

An alternative to the all too common pattern of retirement is *not* to retire but to remain active. You now enjoy a measure of independence with reasonable financial security. And, you possess a considerable competence along with experience and good judgment. You are free to engage in one or several of a variety of interesting and challenging activities on your own terms. Do so.

Reflect that there is no such thing as a permanent vacation. A vacation (by definition) needs to be related to a regular, required, or habitual activity from which the vacation is a break, an interruption, a rest, a respite, an interlude. Constant "loafing" and "taking it easy" would, in contrast, demand a vacation of concentrated, purposeful *work*. Always having nothing that has to be done becomes unbearably boring. It is thought of as great fun. Actually, it is not, except for those who work long and hard—and only for a limited time even for them.

Men and women used to hard concentrated work and demanding challenges, to the stress of competition, and to the pressure of deadlines for many years, cannot adapt well to idleness. For them, having nothing to do and doing nothing will result in both physical and mental deterioration. The sudden and complete relaxation of long-time moderate tension and pressures is not healthy. The body, mind, and temperament have lived with them for so long a time that they are a dominant characteristic of the busy person—what makes him or her "tick." Why not then keep on being active and thereby healthy and happy?

There is a special benefit in being active in your retired years not found in the activity of the years of full employment before retirement. It is well illustrated by a personal experience. A former colleague, spending several days with me, remarked on leaving, "Gosh, you were a very busy man before you retired, but you seem to be doing even more now and to be still enjoying it!"

To which I replied, "Yes, perhaps so. But there is one very important difference—I'm the only boss!"

Being your own boss, no matter how busy you are, is a great relaxer of tensions and pressures.

"Remember that you are retired," "at your age you are doing too much," and variations of those admonitions are heard frequently. It raises the question of what is "too much." This is, of course, an individual matter. Not enough for one can easily be too much for another. A good, generally applicable, criterion might be this: "too much" is when one or more of your activities worries you; when you are much concerned if you can do the job, or if what you did or did not do was right; if you meet your responsibilities with reluctance or outright annoyance; when you have doubts; when it "gets to you." It is not a matter of numbers of things you do or the nature of what you do. It is the ease and satisfaction with which you cope with them.

So, do what you want to, what interests you, so long as it does not "bug you."

Achievement is one of this life's greatest satisfactions. Before retiring, achievement—meeting operating, production, sales and financial quotas, objectives, and goals—was a constant concern towards which all effort was directed. Achievement was the essence of success, of survival. The effort to achieve was a primary motivation; it was stimulating, it was necessary. It can, and should, remain so during one's retired years. And there is the advantage of setting your own objectives, your own goals—and making them as difficult or as easy to attain as *you* want. Achievement, under such circumstances, can be especially satisfying.

If you set yourself too great a challenge, you can always, at any time that suits you, give yourself a vacation!

The alternative to loafing and taking it easy is to remain active, to continue to meet challenges and solve problems and attain objectives. You will, I believe, find that alternative more satisfying, more rewarding, and more fun.

Since our human lives must end eventually, we may say also that it is more satisfying, rewarding, and fun to wear out than it is to rust out or fade away.

The following chapters cover in some detail the various aspects of an active retirement.

3 *Frame of Reference*

Retirement attitudes and activities are influenced strongly by several factors and by your situation prior to retirement. These influences will be reflected in those attitudes and activities unless, of course, you make a determined effort to alter them. So, before proceeding to the larger subjects of attitudes, values, and activities, it may be well first to set down briefly the situations and conditions which provide the background for them.

Your Job Prior to Retirement

Broadly, the situation is one of two.

1) You retire from an important position, successful professional practice, or other independent business effort in which you earn a substantial income. In this instance you are dedicated to your occupation, give little if any thought to retirement (even as it approaches), stay on as long as you can, and actually don't really want to retire. When you do retire, you remain wedded to your former occupation and your former associations and are ill prepared to develop interests in new areas or take on new responsibilities. You tend to look, think, and live in the past—unless you take positive measures to combat and defeat these tendencies.

2) You retire as early as you can afford to from your "necessary" occupation so that you can do what you *really* want to do. In this context, many (if not always recognized) have a

thorough dislike of conventional business of any kind, suffering it as the only practical way to support their families until they can farm, raise horses or cattle, start a mink ranch, engage in archaelogical exploration or some other activity which challenges and pleases them. Such occupations would have been embraced earlier except that they were not sufficiently remunerative.

This adds up to whether or not you had a broad range of interests in your "committed" years, regardless of how engrossed you were in the occupation which provided your living, and how challenging and rewarding it was.

Your Retirement Income

The income you can expect (without working) on retirement will have a major impact on where you will live, how much and how far you will travel, whether or not you "work" to provide necessary supplemental income, to what extent you can be and become active through investment of not only your money but your time and effort and, of course, the extent to which you can afford to take financial risks. That income also affects your attitude toward living in retirement, your feeling of security, your independence, and control of your life style.

Your Plans for Retirement, or Lack of Any

Either you had plans for your retirement or you had not—or you may have had some vague partial plan.

The usual pattern, especially among the occupationally dedicated, is to postpone retirement plans until retirement. It is never too late for anything, but this gets close to it.

Your Age

A mandatory retirement age is today a usual requirement of nearly all corporations and government agencies. Many permit earlier retirement with reduced retirement compensation. Retirement for disability with modified compensation is normal. If you own your business or are otherwise self-employed, the choice of when to retire is, of course, yours. While there are always exceptions, it appears that the age at which people retire is very largely between fifty and seventy.

The age at which you retire will, in many cases, affect your attitudes toward and in retirement—and your desires and abilities. However, you need to put age itself in proper perspective. (More on this in a following chapter.)

Your Health

This may be the most controlling factor in the nature, success, and satisfaction of your retirement and, with age, often the one least subject to your control. The variables are how well you have maintained your health prior to retirement and how fortunate you have been in avoiding crippling diseases and accidents, and how well you have coped with misfortune.

Friends and Close Acquaintances

The extent to which you consider it important to remain in close touch with your friends and acquaintances will affect where you live and what you do when you are retired. A collateral factor is the extent to which you have confidence in your ability to make new friends and find new acquaintances as interesting as those you have, and the extent to which you see this as no problem, or consider it a matter of no concern. In the category of friends and acquaintances you need to—and no doubt have or will—include family.

Where You Live

Where you live prior to retirement will perhaps be the greatest influence on where you live in retirement. You may have a strong desire to stay where you are, or an equally powerful urge and determination to move.

Since the other factors outlined in this chapter have already influenced where you live, these same factors—little changed or substantially modified—will, of course, continue to influence where you live.

In view of these several important, varied, and basic influences on where you will live in retirement, this becomes a major decision.

Your Desire and Ability to Remain Active

Assuming you were active in your job up to the time of your retirement, you then have the ability to live actively in retirement. The strength of your *desire* to remain active will, therefore, largely determine the nature of your retirement. On the other hand, you may view retirement as the long-cherished opportunity to shed all responsibility—to fish, play golf, sail, read, visit old friends, just "take it easy." *You* have that choice. And *you* must make it.

4   *Attitudes*

It is well known (if little respected in practice) that attitude is very important in shaping our values, our motivation, our efforts, our accomplishments, and our satisfactions—and, therefore, in a word, our happiness.

For an example, the actions you take, the way you do things, will be very different depending on whether you view a situation as 10 percent *bad* or 90 percent *good*—whether you believe you can or can't lick City Hall; whether you view the larder as half empty or half full; whether or not you believe that if winter comes, spring is not far behind; that if things are very bad, they can only get better; whether it is your disposition to *try* to do something or to *do* it, to await a change or initiate it, to "wait and see" or to find out.

You can regard retirement from two fundamental and very different viewpoints.

1) As a well and properly earned reward for long and faithful service and a welcome release from the "bondage" of wage (or salary) slavery. This attitude of welcome release is accompanied by a view of retirement as the opportunity to relax by doing nothing—to loaf, sleep late, take a long time over meals, watch the daytime TV programs formerly denied by your occupational "bondage," to catch up on your reading, to fish and play golf. It does seem appealing. And it is the traditional and general attitude.

The fact is that this routine will prove to be thoroughly boring; you will begin to feel sorry for yourself, develop ailments, and soon die from sheer boredom!

The foregoing viewpoint—welcome release from bondage and the well-deserved opportunity to loaf—is that of the end, the finish, the completion of useful activity. It encourages thinking and conversation about what and who *was*.

2) As the third phase of one's living. (The first is your school days. The second, your necessary occupation to earn a living.) This third is the period of true "free-lancing," of uncommitted activity, the opportunity to engage in the occupation of *your* choice on *your* terms. This third phase of your life may actually be much more active than your so-called active career. But there is a great and significant difference—*you* are the boss, the *only* boss!

If you want an active retirement, your primary controlling attitude needs to be that you are, in fact, remaining active, occupied, producing, contributing, only in a different and broader way.

When "Occupation?" appears on the many forms you are asked to fill in, instead of noting "Retired," how satisfactory, how reassuring, how correct it is to write instead, "Consultant," "Farm (or Ranch) Owner-Manager," "Public Relations (or Personnel) Representative," "Author," "Photographer," "Sales Manager," "Chairman, Important County Republican (or Democratic) Committee," "Research Analyst," and what not of this nature.

There is, however, another, a very unhappy and depressing view of retirement. It is associated with mandatory retirement at a specified age. This attitude is one of self-pity and resentment. It views retirement (mandatory) as being discarded, pushed aside as useless, "turned out to pasture" prematurely. This is nonsense.

The establishment of an age at which retirement is mandatory by industry, business, and government should be viewed only as a means of assuring progression, providing increased employment and promotion opportunity, providing for new viewpoints and procedures, and for rewarding those who have given long and faithful service. Mandatory retirement does not mean or imply that at a certain age one is no longer useful, that he is washed up or burned out; it means only that he has served his term and that others should be given an opportunity. The president of our United States, no matter how young or how able, can serve only two terms; the governors of several states are not permitted to succeed themselves; vestries of the Episcopal Church are limited to three-year terms and many clubs and societies have limitations on the incumbency of their officeholders. These limitations have nothing to do with age or ability.

I recall a distinguished business executive saying to me, "If two equally capable managers were being considered for the presidency of my company, and one was forty years old, the other fifty-five, I would select the older, fifty-five year old man."

"Why?" I asked.

"To assure healthy progression in our organization," he replied and continued, "the fifty-five-year-old will only be in office ten years under our sixty-five year old retirement plan and that will give us, within a reasonable length of time, another opportunity for promotion right down the line. The forty year old man would block all higher level promotions for twenty-five years. That's too long."

If you are young at age sixty-five, take retirement in stride and tackle a new job, a new career, and new situations with the same vigor, enthusiasm, confidence, and success with which you pursued the job you just left.

If you are required to retire at a specified age or because you have reached the limit of service, do not feel sorry for yourself. Rather, consider this expected situation an opportunity to take on new activities on your own terms!

Your attitude toward aging is very important in retirement. You must know that you can grow older without being old; that chronological age need not conform to biological age. You must remember, too, that on any day, including anniversaries, you are only a day older than the day before—and also that each day is the first day of the rest of your life!

How old you are depends not on the chronological years you

have been on this earth. It depends on how active, healthy, interested, forward looking, confident, and alert you are. Some are old at forty—others, young at seventy-five. Age is relative; and so is aging. Remaining young, in addition to exerting the effort to remain physically fit, mentally alert, and usefully active, is very largely a matter of a positive attitude. It is a matter of concentrating on the much to be done today and tomorrow, a vigorouis approach to problems, a pleasure in helping others, a zest for living.

Alex Comfort, author of *The Joy of Sex* and *A Good Age*, says:

"The human brain does not shrink, wilt, perish or deteriorate with age. It normally continues to function well through as many as nine decades.

"Most of the handicaps of being old in our society are social, conventional and imaginary. The physical changes are trifling by comparison.

"Older, fit drivers are the least dangerous on the road. By seventy-plus you have experience and have developed a reasonable caution along with confidence; the accident-prone portion of the population is dead or disqualified."

Somewhere, recently, I came upon the following which expresses my views well. It is about the quality of youth. I don't know who the author is or from which magazine I clipped it some few years ago.

Youth is not a time of life, it is a state of mind, a product of the imagination, a vigor of the emotions, a predominance of courage over timidity—an appetite for adventure. Nobody grows old by living a number of years. People grow old when they desert their ideals. Years wrinkle the skin but to give up enthusiasm wrinkles the soul. Worry, self-doubt, fear, anxiety —these are the culprits that bow the head and break the spirit. Whether sixteen or seventy, there exists in the heart of every person who loves life the thrill of a new challenge, the insatiable appetite for what is coming next. You are as young as your faith and as old as your doubts. So long as your heart receives from your head messages that reflect beauty, courage, joy and excitement, you are young. When your thinking becomes clouded with pessimism and prevents you from taking risks, then you are old—and may God have mercy on your soul.

Another important attitude in retirement is to appreciate the ability, knowledge, experience, tolerance, and judgement you have gained. And with this to feel that it is your responsibility to assess opportunities and to continue to use these assets. This combination of qualities is a valuable commodity, since relatively few have it uncommitted. It is, therefore, of concern to you that your special capabilities not be permitted to deteriorate.

Making your unusual and unrestricted talents available to others in new and different enterprises comes close to being an obligation.

Above all, do not dwell on, or even concern yourself with, the good old days, the good old times, and the good old guys and gals. They have gone—and there is so much to do and enjoy now, today, and tomorrow. It might be well to remember, too, that twenty years from now, *these* will be "the good old days."

So, start your retirement by looking upon it as an opportunity for a fresh start, another career, to develop new interests or reestablish old ones, for active involvement in community projects.

And vow to remain young through continuing to exercise your body and your mind, looking ahead and paying no attention to your age.

Remember, too, that you have a lot of ability and that continuing to *use* your talents will prevent their getting rusty and eventually useless.

Finally, convince yourself that there is more fun in wearing out than in rusting out.

5　*Values*

One's values—the things that are important and mean much, that demand a lot of time, effort, and thought, are determined by many things and change from time to time, again for a variety of reasons.

Factors which determine one's values include: age; experiences of childhood; family upbringing and influence; one's school, church, clubs and other social, civic, patriotic, and military organizations; one's business, profession, or other means of livelihood; labor union membership; the extent of one's travel and education; and the breadth of one's youthful and mature experiences. In addition, the amount and nature of one's reading, radio listening, and television viewing are influential in establishing personal values. All of the foregoing contribute, but personal values are influenced most by one's peer group—small and large.

There are marked differences in the values of various groups. For example: between the professions and businessmen on one hand and laborers and "blue collar" workers on the other; and, although to a lesser extent, between attorneys, doctors, and military officers and professors and students.

There are also differences in values among the individuals of a group. These, however, are in the nature of differences in emphasis and order, rather than in the basic values themselves.

The greatest difference in values is between a broad grouping of the relatively young and the relatively older. The young, as opposed to older, are different in physical qualities and temperament. They have, naturally, greater strength and endurance; they react quickly with little thought, are impulsive and impatient, very competitive, over sure of themselves, and tend to be unduly biased. Oldsters make up for the lack of energy, strength and endurance through the application of their greater experience and knowledge, by being more patient, understanding, and less prejudiced, and by weighing and considering carefully the facts before drawing conclusions and making decisions.

So what are, in general, the values of those beginning and moving ahead in their careers as opposed to those reaching their peak—say from ages twenty-five to forty-five or fifty? They would seem to be these: success, wealth, social acceptance, accolades-honors-awards, status symbols, appearance, a degree of independence, doing "one's own thing"; possessions.

Success. Concern in this area is concentrated on advancement in his or her occupation, being elected an officer at least, or president, of the civic, professional, church, social, sports, and other clubs and societies of which he or she is a member. Wealth is, of course, comparative and relative. What most people in the most active years of their occupations want is substantially more than they have. When they reach that plateau, they want to continue to climb higher. Some, but relatively few, set objectives in terms of dollar amounts—$100,000 annual income, or $200,000, or capital of $1 million. And all want to earn as much as their peers.

Social acceptance means being a member of *the* group in the community and being a member of the "right" clubs and social and community organizations, and sending one's children to the "right" schools. Honors of any kind are sought and valued. These would range from "young man of the year," "mother of the year," or councilman to photographs in the local newspaper, mention on the radio, or one's name in print. Status symbols include living in the "right" section of town or the "correct" suburban area, being friendly with the leading influential families, dressing conservatively in the current fashion, driving a good car —kept in good condition and clean—and other such symbols of success. The accumulation of possessions runs on through the years: furniture, appliances, clothes, sports equipment, silver, china and glass, books, objects d'art, and what-not. New items continually increase rather than replace the inventory.

The young and youthful pay little attention to health. Because their health remains good despite misuse by overeating, fad diets to reduce, too much drinking of both alcoholic, carbonated, and sweet concoctions, smoking, and by either exercising not enough or regularly or overexerting for short and separated periods. They believe they will always be healthy.

In contrast, those who are retired and those about to be have other major concerns (values). Briefly these are four: (1) Engagement in a useful activity—being needed, wanted; (2) Having friends and acquaintances; (3) Financial security—assurance that there will be enough money to pay the bills as against amassing a fortune or earning a "lot" of money, and; (4) Good health.

Retired older people are no longer concerned about wealth or increasing income (except, of coure, to meet the ravages of inflation) or success. By now they have, with always some few exceptions, attained the income and success their capabilities permitted. Social acceptance—the "right" people and clubs—honors, awards, and status symbols are now of little importance compared to what these were in the highly competitive younger years.

Appearance to many is still reasonably important—but fashion is not. As for "doing one's own thing," that outstanding characteristic of youth has long gone. One finds a reasonable conformity, with independence, more comfortable. (And one will have learned that the studied non-conformist is among the greatest conformists.)

When one retires he or she has, despite many moves, acquired rooms (and an attic and cellar) full of all kinds of valuable, treasured, and useless possessions. Soon after retirement, with the time and opportunity to do so, one develops a passion to be rid of them.

A simple table of the change in values from those in the most active of their earning years to those of the retired years might be helpful.

"Young" and Active	*Retired*
Success	Useful Activity
Wealth	Financial Security
Social Acceptance	Friends, Acquaintances
Appearance	Still Important
Accolades-Honors-Awards	Little If Any Concern
Status Symbols	No Concern
Doing One's Own Thing	No Concern
Possessions—Building Up	Reducing
No Concern about Health	Good Health

The retired—and those about to be—might well reflect on their values and order them. Then they should concentrate their thinking, planning, and action on the thus established priorities.

6   Keeping Physically Fit and in Good Health

Everyone, old and young, wants to be healthy, along with wanting to be happy and wealthy. The young pay little attention to it, since they are naturally healthy without effort in that direction. Even those who knowingly abuse their healthy bodies and minds with too much of too many drugs, with an unacceptable amount of alcohol, and with tobacco smoke, still seek good health in fields unrelated to their harmful habits.

Whereas wealth does not depend upon good health and actually is in no way directly related to it, the full enjoyment of one's wealth is certainly facilitated by being in good health. Substantial wealth often permits one to buy some portion of certain aspects of good health—medical specialists, sophisticated devices, expensive medicines and treatments, visits to distant and expensive places.

That good health contributes significantly to being happy needs no comment.

Good health is evident in a firm handclasp; standing and sitting erect; chin up and looking ahead; walking with a long, firm, springy stride ("He looks as if he knows where he's going."); eyes bright and sparkling; an understanding smile; an interested and attentive manner; an air of assurance and confidence; a lean and muscular body.

Acquiring and maintaining these characteristics of fitness requires thought, orderly planning, and a great deal of determined doing. They are not going to just happen.

Seven Basic Elements

There are seven basic elements of acquiring and maintaining good health, of becoming and remaining physically fit. These are:
Diet
Exercise

Good posture
Deep breathing
Mental composure—Looking ahead
Self-confidence
Periodic physical examinations

The first two—proper diet and sufficient and correct exercise—are quite familiar. Much has been written, said, and demonstrated about these two important elements. On the other hand, the public has been made only a little aware of the importance of breathing deeply and hardly aware at all of the great importance of good posture. It is not difficult to find innumerable badly stoop-shouldered men and women carefully watching their diets and exercising regularly while they "sit on their backs."

A healthy body needs a healthy mind and vice versa. But little has been said or written in the area of general health about the importance of a good attitude, a cheerful outlook, a relatively unworried mind, mental composure, or self-confidence.

The importance of regular physical examinations is generally recognized, but the procedure is more often than not respected in the failure to have one.

Diet

A number of very good books have been written on the related subjects of diet and nutrition. They go into considerable detail, report the results of research, relate experience, and illustrate with examples. They describe body functioning, chemical action, the digestive process, the contribution (or lack of it) of a large number of "foods" to normal and desirable body functions, to one's weight, and to good health. They contain tables and lists of foods with the calories and grams, protein, carbohydrate, fat, and roughage contents of each and other such scientific data.

Since so much detailed scientific information on nutrition and diet is so readily available, and since I have no training in medicine, nutrition, or diet, I will cover these subjects briefly, and directly from the layman's viewpoint—what I believe you and I should know about diet and nutrition.

What you and I should know about nutrition and diet is much like what we should know about our automobile. We need to know how to use it and care for it in order to keep it in satisfactory, efficient working order for a long time at the least expense. When serious trouble occurs beyond our comprehension and ability to repair, we turn our car over to an experienced and reliable mechanic.

You and I want to know what kind of gasoline to use and how much mileage we should expect; the best kind of oil to use and how often to change it; what kind and quantity of antifreeze to put in the radiator; the correct pressure for each tire and how often to check it; the most efficient speed; means of prolonging the life and efficiency of the battery; how often we should have our car greased; how often the spark plugs should be cleaned and changed. Knowing the details of how the motor and transmission operate; the location and operation of the various electric circuits; the various stages of compression, combustion, firing, and exhaust; understanding the transmission system and differential action of the axles and wheels—all of this would certainly be interesting. It is, however, dubiously useful.

Now back to nutrition and diet. The building blocks of amino acids; the function of the liver and kidneys, large and small intestines, the spleen and gall bladder; the chemical actions which take place in the stomach, intestines and bloodstream; the functions, absorption, and elimination of cholesterol; the interaction of salt and water in the body and other such biological and anatomical matters are, again, surely interesting but of little, if any, practical value. And if such limited knowledge should result in self-treatment, it might be positively harmful. A little knowledge may indeed be dangerous. In any event, these are not the things you and I want to know about nutrition and diet. Nor can we understand them without a great deal of study.

What is it then that the layman—you and I—wants to know and, in any event, should know about his diet and nutrition?

Basically we should know which foods best provide needed nutrition and required energy, in what quantities, and in what balance or mix. And we should know some limited basic facts about nutrition and diet.

This broad objective may, in turn, be subdivided this way:

(1) An overall and simplistic understanding of the four basic classifications of human foods and what they contribute to good health, and the three basic chemical elements of food and their contribution.
(2) The basic principles of a healthy, nutritious diet.
(3) Which foods you should eat and what you should drink for good health and in what quantities and balance.
(4) Which foods and drinks you had best avoid.
(5) What dietary supplements (vitamins and minerals) are healthy—and in what quantities.

We will now enlarge a little on each of these subdivisions.

1. The Background of Nutrition and Diet

Food is usually divided into four basic groups:

a. Meats (beef, lamb, pork, and some undomesticated animals); fowl or poultry (chicken, turkey, duck, pigeon, quail, and others); and fish (in large variety—ocean, deep sea, lake, river, hard-shell and soft).
b. Dairy products—milk, butter, and cheese in many varieties.
c. Fruits and vegetables—fresh, canned, processed, and dried.
d. Grains—natural and included in cereals and breads.

All contain and provide some vitamins and minerals, but each contributes primarily one of the three basic elements outlined in the following:

a. The meat, poultry, and fish group is high in *protein.*
b. Dairy products are also high in protein and in carbohydrates, (calories to provide energy,) and provide meaningful quantities of needed calcium, phosphorus, and vitamins A and B-2.
c. Fruits and vegetables, especially when fresh, provide energy, vitamins A and C, and calcium and phosphorus.
d. Cereals and "natural" breads provide energy, a little protein, and needed vitamins and minerals.

Food is also classified with respect to the three basic nutritional elements it provides. These are:

a. *Protein,* which provides additional and replacement tissue for the growth and maintenance of the body and its functions.

b. *Carbohydrates* (starches and sugars), which supply energy (measured in calories) and needed roughage.
c. *Fats* (oil and grease), which also supply energy and aid the solution and retention of some vitamins and minerals.

If you consume carbohydrates and fats in excess of what is required to meet your energy needs, the excess is stored in your body as fat.

If, on the other hand, you do not consume enough carbohydrates and fats to produce the calories for the physical energy you expend, your body will draw on any stored fat and on your protein intake.

The *balance* among the foods you eat is usually expressed in the relative number of grams (weight) contained in each component.

The *amount* of food you eat—and plan to eat and should eat—is expressed in both grams (weight) and in *calories*, a measure of its energy-producing value (in terms of heat).

Vitamin and mineral supplements are, in addition, generally listed as a percentage of recommended average daily adult requirement, where this had been determined.

On the average and in general, as a rough guide:

A man aged sixty to seventy, weighing about 155 pounds and standing about five feet, nine inches tall and reasonably active should consume, daily, food providing about 2,200 to 2,400 calories and 70 grams of protein.

A woman aged sixty to seventy, weighing about 130 pounds and about five feet, four inches tall and reasonably active should consume, daily, food containing about 1,600 to 1,800 calories and 58 grams of protein.

2. Basic Principles of a Healthy and Nutritious Diet

a. Eat *three* meals a day, including a substantial breakfast.
b. Drink a large glass of *water* the first thing in the morning and just before going to bed—and *before* each meal. You should, on the average, consume eight glasses per day. (There is an amount of water in the foods we eat, especially in fresh fruits and vegetables.)

c. Add *no salt* to the food served to you at the table. Many natural foods and nearly all prepared, processed, and cooked foods contain an adequate—usually ample—amount of salt. Substitute spices for flavor instead of salt.

d. Use fresh lemon juice and vegetable oil (with a little vinegar) as a salad dressing.

e. Avoid pepper and "hot" spices.

f. Finish your meal before you are filled; leave the table feeling that you could eat a little more. (The best exercise to control your weight is to push away from the table!)

g. Chew your food thoroughly; eat slowly.

h. Use vegetable margarine in cooking instead of butter.

i. Include some of each of the four basic food groups (meat, poultry, fish; fruit and vegetables; dairy products; cereals) in each day's meals.

j. Include each day all of the nutrient elements—protein, carbohydrates, polyunsaturated fats—and some fiber or roughage, but keep the carbohydrates and fats in low proportion to the protein in terms of both grams of weight and calories of energy. Include a high porportion of fresh fruits and/or vegetables and a small quantity of nuts or dried fruit.

k. Determine from your doctor, a nutritionist, or dietician, or from your own experience, the number of calories your three daily meals should provide—in view of your normal activities, your body's absorption and use of food, and the state of your health—and also the grams of protein, carbohydrates, and fat required. Then plan your diet to conform.

l. Do not indulge in between-meal and before-bedtime snacks. If, on occasions, you must, eat fresh celery, carrots, unsalted nuts, bits of cheddar cheese, raisins, and dried fruit.

3. Foods to Eat

The foods you should eat to achieve and maintain good health embrace a large number and variety. Nearly all of the published books on nutrition and diet have some sixteen to twenty-four pages listing all the foods you and I have eaten and know of, stating the number of calories they contain as well as the number of protein, carbohydrate and fat grams, vitamins, and minerals.

There would appear to be little use in duplicating such lists here. Broadly and in general, the types of food which will provide sufficient but not excess calories and an adequate number of grams of protein are these:

a. Lean meat, skinless poultry, the less oily fish and shellfish—broiled, baked, boiled or raw—but not fried.
b. Fresh fruits of all kinds and most vegetables, but go light on avocados and olives. Boiled and baked vegetables (especially soybeans), but go light on potatoes and corn.
c. Some dairy products—cottage, American, cheddar, cream and swiss cheeses, evaporated and skimmed milk, very little butter (a pat a day).
d. Natural cereals, "natural" breads, and wheat germ.
e. In small quantities, most nuts, raisins, dried fruits, vegetable oils (for salad dressing).

The foregoing permits you a large choice and provides considerable variety. In preparing a day's menu, choose from these groups balanced meals consisting of some of all of the groups and then refer to one of the tables of calories and protein grams and compute the total. If the calories exceed your requirements (say over 2,400) or the protein grams are not sufficient (say only fifty), then substitute other foods which will cause the total day's consumption to reach your objectives. Tables of calories and grams are available in inexpensive paperback books in most bookshops.

As a guide there follows a balanced daily menu of about 2,200 calories and 70 protein grams—shown separately for breakfast, lunch, and dinner.

Breakfast (Make it a hearty one, since you have had nothing to eat for close to twelve hours and will not have another meal for four hours or more.)

Group A: Fresh fruit, citrus—orange, grapefruit; or
               Fresh fruit, noncitrus—apple, pear, peach, berries, grapes, cherries, mango, papaya, banana; or
               Cooked and dried fruit—prunes, raisins, apricots.
Group B: Fruit and vegetable juices—orange, grapefruit, prune, cranberry, tomato.
Group C: Cereal with milk—the "natural" kind; add a table-

spoonful of wheat germ and a tablespoonful of raisins, if not included.

Group D: An egg—boiled or poached, occasionally fried, scrambled or omeletted in margarine; or a slice of lean meat or fowl, or a small portion of baked or broiled fish; or a small portion of cheddar or cottage cheese.

Group E: One slice of natural grain bread, toasted, with one pat of margarine.

Group F: A glass of milk or a cup of weak tea (no milk, cream, or sugar), or a cup of sanka or decaffinated coffee (no milk, cream, or sugar).

Include one of the items in each group. This is a "big" breakfast—fruit, fruit juice, cereal, and egg or protein substitute, a slice of toast, and a beverage. Doctors will tell you that you should have a "good" ("big") breakfast.

Lunch (Two triskets, but no bread)

Group A: A salad—chicken, fish, vegetable, tomato (alone), fruit, cottage cheese and fruit, "chef's"—with lemon juice and a vegetable oil and vinegar dressing.

Group B: Sardines, salmon, a small portion of broiled or baked fish with a green vegetable or tomatoes.

Group C: A slice of lean meat, poultry, broiled chopped steak, or cottage cheese with a green vegetable or tomatoes.

Group D: Beef or tomato bouillon—hot or jellied—or fruit or vegetable juice.

Group E: Fresh citrus or noncitrus fruit—whole, sliced, or wedges.

Group F: A glass of milk or a cup of weak tea (no milk, cream, or sugar), or a cup of sanka or decaffinated coffee (no milk, cream, or sugar), or iced tea, sanka, or decaffinated coffee (no milk, cream, or sugar).

Include one of the items in either Group A, B or C, and one of the items in Group F—this is a light lunch which is what most of us should have. Add one of the items in Groups D or E, or both, if your weight and exercise scheduled permit.

Dinner (No bread)

Group A: Two slices of lean meat or poultry, or a medium portion of baked or broiled fish with a green or yellow vegetable and a small baked, boiled, or roasted potato.

Group B: A small fruit, vegetable, tomato, or cottage cheese and fruit salad with lemon juice and vegetable oil and vinegar dressing.

Group C: A cup of weak tea, sanka, or decaffinated coffee (no milk, cream, or sugar).

Group D: Fresh citrus or noncitrus fruit, or gelatin—or cheddar or cream cheese on four whole wheat or trisket-type crackers.

Group E: Beef or tomato bouillon—hot or jellied—or fruit or vegetable juice.

Include one the items in Groups A, B and C. Add one of the items in Groups D or E, or both, if your weight, exercise schedule, and doctor's advice permit.

4. Foods to Avoid Eating

candy
pies and tarts
doughnuts, cake, cookies
buns, biscuits, rolls, muffins, white bread
pancakes, griddle cakes
ice cream
meat fat and fatty meats
fowl and fish skin
frankfurters, sausage, bacon
foods fried—especially deep fried—in fat, lard and butter
gravies (except natural meat juice), sauces, dressing (except oil and vinegar).
potato chips, popcorn, pretzels
butter and cream
added salt (to what is already present naturally or in cooking)
sugar on cereals and fruit and in beverages
separate vitamin A and D tablets—unless ordered by your doctor

and drinking:

colas and other carbonated and sweetened beverages
beer and sweet wines
alcoholic drinks mixed with anything but water

It is best to eat (and drink) none of the foregoing, ever. However, if, occasionally to avoid embarrassing your host or guests, you eat and drink some of these in small quantities, no great harm is done.

5. Dietary Supplements

If your menus reasonably follow the prescriptions in this chapter—liberal in fresh fruits and vegetables, and meeting the protein requirements—you should need little if any vitamin and mineral supplements. However, as a precaution and for added assurance that you are ingesting all of the needed vitamins and minerals in at least the recommended daily adult requirements, you might well take daily an all-purpose, multivitamin and mineral capsule. A good formula of this type, sold in many drugstores at varying prices, will be found in the following section headed "Vitamins and Minerals."

Exercise

The key to physical fitness is physical activity—sustained and low level, like walking briskly, jogging, running, bicycling, swimming. And the greatest cause of and reason for aging is inactivity. Our bodies thrive on being used.

Your body needs exercise for a variety of purposes: to strengthen your muscles and to keep them elastic, resilient (including, of course, your heart); to increase the flow of blood to your organs, muscles and skin; to stimulate processes for the elimination of bodily waste; to utilize the full capacity of your lungs; to achieve a good body tone.

Regular exercise has other beneficial effects. It prevents development of high blood pressure and diabetes, relieves nervous tension and lessens fatigue; it helps you lose weight and stay slim; it helps you look better, feel better, think better, and do better.

To provide energy, your body burns up the calories (supplied by the food you eat) not needed for repair and maintenance. This burning is done by hard physical work or exercise. Otherwise the excess calories are stored as fat. Driving a car, working, however hard, at a desk, and thinking even the greatest thoughts are not physical activity and burn few calories. Older bodies burn the calories less efficiently than younger bodies.

Physical activity, exercise, is essential to good health and to physical fitness at any age. It is especially important as one grows older and tends, naturally, to be less physically active and, in most cases, to lead a largely sedentary life.

The organs which need exercise most to sustain physical, and thereby also mental, fitness are the heart (our most important muscle), the lungs, and the blood vessels. Other muscles need conditioning and tone through sustained physical work and/or exercise, but of primary importance is the cardiovascular-respiratory system. Exercise and physical activity should therefore be directed primarily toward strengthening that basic system—and to avoiding harm to it.

From middle age on—and retired people fall into this category —exercise (and physical activity) should be, as noted previously, constant and at a low level of exertion—walking briskly, jogging, running, bicycling, swimming. And such exercises should be taken with regularity and with only slowly increasing intensity. One should devote a minimum of fifteen minutes a day to his or her exercises; even better, an hour.

Exercises which largely contract muscles suddenly for short periods of time and require vigorous physical exertion—pushing, pulling, lifting—causing sudden high blood pressure and markedly increased heart beat—should be strictly avoided. Such activity—carrying heavy loads, moving furniture, pushing a stalled car, shoveling snow, weight-lifting exercises—are very apt to cause a heart attack. Exercise should increase the *flow* of blood, not increase blood *pressure*. In any case, if you follow a brilliant career as a young champion athlete with a successful career at a desk, do *not*, twenty years later, attempt to indulge in physical exertion as if you were still that twenty-year-ago brilliant athlete. It may kill you!

By the same token, avoid "crash" programs—the exercise ones are as ineffective and harmful as the dietary variety—and avoid *over* exertion. What is *over* exertion will vary among individuals and, for any individual, with the level of fitness.

Let us now return to effective exercise. A physical fitness program for persons over fifty years old should start with a brisk walk daily of about fifteen minutes duration. At first walk on relatively flat ground. Work up to including slopes of increasing steepness and walking both faster and for a longer period. If this exercise is effective, you should be "out of breath" (panting or puffing) about half the time. When your walking exercise causes you no discomfort, you can proceed to jogging.

First, alternate walking and jogging—walking one minute and jogging twenty seconds—for about twenty minutes. Then work up to walking one minute and jogging a minute, for twenty minutes; then walk a minute and jog six minutes, three times. Now gradually move up until you can jog for twelve minutes (about a mile) and walk a mile, twice.

As an approximate guide to pace, you should cover a hundred yards at a walk in a minute; at a jog, in forty seconds.

When you have reached this desirable level of exertion, you may add running, bicycling, and swimming. The amount—distances and time—is best discussed with your doctor. As a rough guide, indulge in these exercises until you *begin* to tire; then taper off.

A note of caution. Jogging and running are excellent for strengthening and conditioning the cardio-vascular system; but this form of exercise may harm your leg and foot bones, their joints and muscles. Consult your doctor about your jogging and running program.

Calisthenics—arm swinging, leg and knee lifts and bending, push-ups, sit-ups, toe touching, torso and neck twists—are good exercises in themselves. In addition, they are beneficial as "warm-up" preparation for walking, running, swimming and related exercises. Following the calisthenics, if you cannot be outdoors, jog in place.

A caution here. Do *not* touch your toes stiff legged. Bend the knees. Do not do sit-ups with your legs stretched out flat. Again, bend your knees. And don't do deep, full knee bends. Bend them only about a quarter of their full capacity.

In general, too, do not run without first walking briskly or jogging a short time, four to six minutes, to permit your heart to absorb the increased heavy work load gradually.

To the extent that it is practicable, do your exercises before breakfast or two hours after a meal, and, in any event, not less than an hour after a meal. If you are not too tired, you may do calisthenic exercises for five or six minutes before going to bed.

When you jog, try to do so on relatively soft ground, grass or leaves, and wear cushioned jogging shoes. These are available at most sporting goods stores.

If you are up to it, and want to exercise by climbing stairs, do so for a continuous period of about ten minutes to derive benefit from the exertion. *Sustained,* low level, unstrained effort is the key; your heart and lungs and blood vessels need time to adjust to the increased demand for energy. Ordinarily, this takes from four to six minutes.

Golf, if you *walk* the whole course, is good exercise and it is pleasurable. It is not, however, nearly as beneficial as briskly walking the same distance.

Tennis, for the middle aged and older, provides good exercise and, if played regularly—say four to six times a week—will contribute effectively to maintaining physical fitness. But it is a strenuous game (doubles is desirable). You must therefore be fit or build up to exertion of that intensity gradually.

Rowing, paddling a canoe, hunting, volleyball are beneficial physical activities, when you are fit for them and can pursue them with reasonable regularity.

Isometric exercises—opposing muscle against muscle and pushing against solid surfaces—have an off-again, on-again vogue because they can be done sitting at a desk, lying in bed, standing, waiting for a bus, and at any time. They are not good for you. They are especially not good for older, sedentary types because the sudden muscular contraction increases blood pressure and increases the heart beat too rapidly.

Massage is good for relaxing and untensing uptight muscles, but contributes little, if anything, to an exercise program.

Workouts in a gymnasium or "conditioning room" at a sports club are beneficial if the activities include riding a stationary bicycle, running on a treadmill, calisthenics, swimming, handball, and squash—if you are fit enough for these relatively demanding games, and provided the routine does not include weight lifting. (Bear in mind that we are writing about the middle-aged and older.)

And remember, if you are overweight, the best exercise is to push away from the table!

The intensity and the difficulty of your exercises are increased by increasing the resistance to your efforts. For example, walking, jogging and running will require more effort if you travel uphill an increasing portion of your route and if you move faster. Likewise, encountering hills on your bicycle rides and peddling faster and tightening the roller pressure on the wheel of a stationary bicycle will take more out of you. It will require more exertion if you slow your push-ups and if you hold a weight on your chest when you do sit-ups.

The scope of this book does not permit outlining the many specific exercise programs for particular purposes and special groups. There is a large number of books outlining them, several by national military establishments and a variety of health organizations.

It is appropriate here, however, to summarize some of the remarks with respect to exercise:

(1) Exercise regularly an hour or more each day.

(2) Exercise vigorously—inducing perspiration, rapid and deep breathing, and an increase in pulse and respiration.

(3) Exercise—as far as practicable—first to strengthen the heart, lungs and blood vessels, and then to produce a balanced muscle development—chest, legs, thighs, arms, back, neck, shoulders. You may need a doctor to advise you on your exercise plan in this respect.

(4) Build up from easy and less demanding exercises to more strenuous and demanding ones gradually and systematically. Again, it is wise to consult your doctor about an effective program.

(5) Be sure that your exercises are not counterproductive—such as touching your toes with knees straight or doing sit-ups with your legs unbent. Done this way these two exercises *stretch* muscles that should be *tightened.* And avoid weight-lifting and isometric-type exercises.

(6) To the extent practicable, assign a portion of your exercise to competitive sports and games (golf, tennis—especially doubles—volleyball, hunting, rowing, canoeing); the interest, changing situation and competition sharpen the mind while also relaxing it, and the body reaps the benefit of rhythm, balance and variety.

(7) Develop an exercise plan and stick to it; include in the plan progressive standards—time, weight, distance, numbers—to be achieved.

Somewhat as afterthoughts, but contributing usefully to good health, are two seldom mentioned ''exercises:''

(1) The *eye* muscles. Look at a distance, then at something very close to you—then look as far to the right as you can without turning your head and then as far to the left as you can, again without turning your head. You can do this while driving, while reading and while walking. Do these exercises at least six times daily.

(2) Chew your food thoroughly—at least thirty times per mouthful. Some many years ago this good practice—known as fletcherizing—was very popular.

We have commented frequently in this section on the importance of regularity in exercise and in maintaining a level of fitness. My observation of talented athletic horses and men indicates that as you grow older, you do not so much lose your physical abilities as you do your recuperative powers.

When you are in your late teens and early twenties, you can play three hard sets of tennis, not play again for two weeks and then repeat the effort. Not so when you are forty-five, fifty, or older. This sort of thing would risk a heart attack. If, however, in your middle and later years, you play tennis nearly every day, the exercise is beneficial. But if you don't keep it up, you may lose the ability forever.

There are many good tennis players whose ages range from seventy-five to over eighty. Of course, they play every day. If one of them does not play for a year, I doubt he will ever play again. I had a remarkable horse some years ago who at the age of twenty-three—equivalent to over ninety in human age—won three gruelling eighteen-mile cross-country events over some twenty "jumps." "Marse Henry" was a remarkable horse his entire long life; he died at the age of twenty-eight because, I believe, the friend in whose care I left him when I went off to the war failed to exercise him as I had requested. His vigor at an advanced age, I feel sure, resulted from the daily two hours of hard work I gave him. But once "let down," there was no way to get him back into top form. So, thin, weak, and out of shape from lack of vigorous exercise, he had to be "put down."

The U.S. Air Force Medical Corps devised a test of physical fitness based on the number of minutes required to run 1½ miles and, conversely, the distance run in twelve minutes. A review of these tests indicates that for those over fifty years of age you are in *good* physical condition if you are able to comfortably run (without undue strain) 1½ miles in fifteen minutes and in *fair* condition if you can run the 1½ miles comfortably in seventeen minutes. Rough equivalents would be the ability to run 1¼ miles (good) and 1 1/8 miles (fair) in twelve minutes.

In summary, to achieve and maintain good health and physical fitness as your age advances, you must remain physically active. You need to combat, to counteract, the natural tendency to slow down and reduce activity. This, in turn, requires disciplined adherence to an appropriate progressive exercise program in accordance with the principles outlined in this section.

With respect to your heart, lungs, blood vessels, limb and stomach muscles—if you don't use them, you will lose them! And it is never to late to be benefitted by exercise—and never too early to begin!

Posture

It is important to stand straight, shoulders back, head erect, weight distributed equally on the feet, knees and hips. And it is important to sit straight; the upper torso as if there were no back to the chair and in the same position as if you were standing straight. Why?

Because correct posture permits all of the internal organs to function properly and freely. Poor posture cramps and restricts them. In addition, correct posture keeps the muscles in their normal relationships of stress, pressures, relaxation, flexibility and rest. Poor posture places constant unnatural strain on the muscles, stretching some that should not be constantly stretched and contracting others more than they should be. And vital organs, because they do not have the room they should have, do not function as they should.

Thus poor posture is not only unattractive, but contributes to poor health as well. It is most often evidenced by stooped shoulders in both men and women (the widow's hump). The stooped shoulders are most often caused by failing to stand straight when standing and slouching (sitting on one's shoulders) when sitting.

The positive action to achieve and maintain good posture is constantly to be aware of good posture and to practice it; to stand straight and to sit straight, well against the back of the chair, and to do back strengthening exercises daily. In extreme cases of stooped shoulders, braces may be helpful.

A happy thought: a good posture will improve your stature!

Deep Breathing

Your lungs, like the muscles in your body, need exercise. They need frequently to be used to their full capacity to remain healthy. Vigorous exercise, strenuous competitive games—climbing, running, jogging, swimming, bicycling, tennis, calisthenics, workouts in a gymnasium—all of these will generally extend the lungs to their full capacity.

Planned, regular exercise will not only tone and strengthen the muscles, but will also tone and strengthen the lungs and heart—the whole circulatory system.

The lungs may also be strengthened and used to full capacity by periodically breathing deeply of fresh air. The exercise is simple. Extending the diaphragm down and outward, breathe in fully to the count of six (or as near to six as you can); hold your breath to the count of six; exhale while drawing the diaphragm in and up, again to the count of six (or as near to that number as you can get). Do this a minimum of four and perferably six times each day during daylight hours outdoors. This exercise is not difficult and if you schedule this minor effort it will soon become a habit. And the good effect on your health will more than make the little effort required well worthwhile.

Attitude and Outlook

A healthy body contributes much to a healthy mind. A healthy body removes a primary worry, produces mental energy, and contributes to a general feeling of well being.

A healthy mind may be defined as one which can cope with and habitually minimizes harassment, worries, concerns, danger, threats, disappointment, defeat, and the several other disagreeable and unsettling situations which constantly confront us in normal, let alone abnormal, living. A healthy mind is one that uses the past only to help predict the present and future; that concentrates on making the good better to reduce the bad (If the bottle is half empty, it is also half *full*; if something is twenty percent bad, it is also eighty percent good!); that recognizes problems and troubles as normal and is concerned primarily with correcting them; that sees the future as a challenge; that attacks a problem with how it can be solved rather than the difficulty of doing so; that accepts with serenity the things that cannot be changed and proceeds with courage to change those it can; and one that has confidence in its ability while recognizing its limitations.

You and Your Doctor

A regular complete physical examination by a doctor is a most important, probably essential, measure to prevent serious health hazards and disability. The cost in time, money, and inconvenience is small compared to the great benefit derived in learning about potential trouble before it develops or becomes serious.

A physical examination every six months is desirable; having one once a year is a necessity to assure maintenance of good health. Your doctor will know if a test for glaucoma and cholesterol in the blood and an electrocardiogram is warranted.

As the result of a periodic examination your doctor will, with few exceptions, recommend some treatment, procedure, or course of action; positive or negative. If you are one of the fortunate few, your doctor may remark, "I don't know all that you do, but whatever it is, keep it up!"

Usually, however, after the examination you will face the real test of your determination to be healthy, to keep fit. The challenge is to follow implicitly your doctor's orders. He may counsel that you stop smoking; eat more or less of this or that; reduce your cocktails to two before dinner (although in some instances, to dilate the blood vessels, he may prescribe an extra drink or two!); that you increase, decrease or modify your exercise program. Whatever it is, it is sure to be difficult. It is your problem. But you must meet the challenge.

Sexual Satisfaction

"Is satisfactory sexual experience—vigor, potency—possible in my older years?" Certainly it is. "Is sexual activity good for me in my older years—is it healthy?" Yes, indeed it is. "I can't seem to do my part. I'm not interested and if I do get the urge, I can't get an erection!" The reason is that you *think* you can't—fear, doubt, concern—and worry about and concentration on other things.

A lot of documented experience indicates that the desire for sexual expression and interest in sexual companionship and the ability to perform well and gain satisfaction need not, and in many cases do not, change with age. With rare exceptions, lack of ardor and impotence found in older men are due to causes other than age.

There is really nothing in sexual desire and performance to deteriorate. The urge for sexual intercourse is natural and basic to survival. Readiness for it is simple—a flow of blood to a vital organ triggered by a mental reflex and stimulation by friction.

The only material change in the sex urge and satisfaction is that one becomes more selective, more particular, not so easily and immediately aroused—because of experience and a wider range of interests largely lacking in youth.

A number of "old wives' tales"—widely held beliefs which have no basis in fact as indicated by scientific investigation and research—are disturbingly current. Accepting these false assertions may prove harmful as well as distressing.

Among the "old wives' tales" are these:

(1) In your late-middle and older years aging causes you to lose sexual ardor and potency; this is natural and to be expected. As stated in a preceding paragraph, scientific evidence indicates that there is no normal relationship between aging and loss of sexual urge and ability.
(2) Sexual activity in one's older years is damaging to one's health. Nonsense—it is actually healthy.

(3) Testosterone and other hormones will restore potency (lost manhood) and maintain sexual ardor and ability. They won't, except as you think they will.
(4) Certain special drugs will restore and increase potency. Almost surely not—unless you think so.
(5) Men, at varying ages, experience a "change of life" similar to the female menopause or climacteric. Since men do not menstruate, the comparison is foolish. But what is meant, no doubt, is that like women, men lose sexual desire and potency. Here again, this is not true of women after the menopause and the comparison seems highly inadvisable. A doctor will tell you that men do *not* experience a "change of life," at any age.

There are, surely, many other disturbing and distressing myths concerning the decline in male sexual ability. Before you accept any of them, consult your doctor as to their soundness.

Everyone, basically and naturally, has a sufficient sex drive, desire, urge, whatever you wish to call it. Variations exist in what it takes to stimulate this drive. A satisfying, pleasant, interesting, exciting, and joyous sex relationship is an art—the art of making love.

Development of this art requires skill, imagination, variety, thought and thoughtfulness, confidence, and above all, a genuine desire to make one's partner happy.

In order to develop the necessary skills and techniques of making love successfully, one must have a knowledge of the male and female genital organs and secondary erotic areas and the techniques of satisfactory sexual intercourse. Many books, several of them excellent, on the subject are readily available. One of them is titled *Sex til Seventy and After* by Franz Halda.

A happy sex relationship makes for good health and peace of mind; a poor one is frustrating and disturbing.

Partners of many years need, more than others, to exercise imagination, variety, patience, and thoughtfulness. If arousing passion takes a little more effort and a bit more time than when you were substantially younger, the pleasure is greater and more lasting.

This rhyme (toast), author unknown, seems appropriate:

May you live as long as you want to,
May you want to as long as you live.
If you do and I don't—make me;
If I sleep and you want to—wake me.
May you live as long as you want to,
May you want to as long as you live!

In the context of this section it seems appropriate also to suggest reference to the old adage: "If you don't use it, you lose it!"

Sleep

Sleep is a necessary requirement and essential function of the human body. Everyone needs *some* sleep in a twenty-four-hour period. How much seems to vary considerably among individuals. The medical profession is attempting to learn more about the phenomenon of sleep.

Perhaps the best guide to the amount of sleep required, if you are in reasonably good health, is to go to bed and to sleep when you are tired (if you can, and *not* when you are driving), and to get up when you awaken refreshed (if your day's activity permits it). If that simple formula is limited by necessary early morning activities, then come as close to it as practicable.

Sleeping a given number of hours, eight is traditional, can become habitual by generally observing a stated bedtime and time of arising. It seems that the body and mind adapt readily to such an orderly regimen.

Naps of varying lengths seem to be beneficial, provided you are in a position to enjoy them. This, again, means dozing off when you feel the need for sleep and awakening naturally and, presumably, refreshed.

If you suffer from insomnia, you need help. Don't take pills, see your doctor.

In a nutshell, develop a natural habit of sleep suited to *you*. Don't coax it with pills. Don't fight it. And if you have trouble sleeping, see your doctor.

Sitting too Long

Most of us want to sit as often and for as long as we can. We want to "get the load off of our feet." This is understandable, but it is not healthy and often not even refreshing.

Phlebitis—a painful and debilitating inflammation of the veins of the legs—comes from sitting for long periods.

In general, try not to sit for more than an hour at a time. At the end of an hour, get out of your chair, walk around a little, take some deep breaths (of fresh air if you can), and then go back to your chair. It won't take long for this routine to become habitual—to the benefit of your health.

Smoking

Smoking tobacco, in whatever form, is harmful. The tar and nicotine one inhales may, and more often than not does cause emphysema, cancer, and a number of other serious diseases—and death.

Observation and experience indicate that one will smoke or not smoke; there is no middle ground. There is no such thing as smoking "a little." And if a smoker wants to stop smoking, he or she must, at a given time, *stop* smoking. You can't "cut down" gradually.

At the age of retirement, either you do not smoke or you are a confirmed habitual smoker. If you want then to stop smoking, you must quit entirely.

Kicking the habit of smoking is one of the most difficult tasks confronting a human. However, it can be done and often has been. It requires considerable courage and great determination— and a very difficult physical, mental, and psychological adjustment. There are several "tricks" effective in accomplishing the change (your doctor can suggest some) but gradually reducing the number of cigarettes one smokes is not one of them.

Smoking—cigarettes, pipes, cigars—is an unhealthy, harmful, dirty, and expensive habit—or better, addiction. If you smoke you ought to attempt to stop doing so.

On the other hand, the number of smokers and number of cigarettes smoked continues to increase each year. And then a substantial number of smokers live to be over eighty years of age and show no pronounced ill effects from their vice. To put the matter in sound perspective, you may reason that you may well stop smoking—at great cost to your favorite and habitual satisfaction—and within a short time die as the result of a motor or aircraft accident, a brick or heavy tree limb falling on your head, blood poisoning, eating contaminated food, and what-not. So why not enjoy yourself?

I suggested to a heavy-smoking friend, "I'm not presuming to tell you to stop smoking, it's *your* life—only that you assess the situation intelligently. Knowing that your smoking is harmful and dangerous to your health, does the pleasure you derive from it make the risk worthwhile? Do the two balance? If your answer is 'yes'—then God bless you, keep on smoking!"

Drinking

Drinking alcoholic beverages of one kind or another has been habitual among humans for thousands of years—through the fermentation and distillation of fruits and grains. Drinking a little of alcoholic beverages—wines, whiskies, beers, and liquors slowly and at well-spaced intervals is generally not harmful and in some cases is actually beneficial. Alcohol dilates the blood vessels.

Too much alcohol, taken too quickly and in a short time, is harmful. This will slow the mind, dislodge logic, blur the speech, dull reaction, coordination and perception, upset the stomach and liver, decrease strength (physical and moral), and do strange things to the emotions; you lose control. You are a threat of danger to others as well as to yourself.

The effect of alcohol on mind and muscle varies considerably among individuals; tolerances vary widely. At the age most retire, each has established an alcohol-drinking pattern; each knows his or her limits and the effects. There would appear, generally, no need to change habits in this area developed over many years.

But there is a concern, a danger, the retiree should recognize. Not as active as prior to retirement and with perhaps less need to have no alcohol on one's breath, idleness and some loneliness may easily encourage a ''nip'' more often than previously and a bit larger and stronger drink as one settles down before the TV tube.

Beware! Don't let drinking become a problem. And, if it already is one, you have more time to ''kick it!''

Cholesterol

A few years ago, in Detroit, I was taking my breakfast in the hotel dining room. I had ordered grapefruit, a dry cereal, liver and bacon, one piece of natural wheat toast, and hot tea with lemon. As I was about to start on the liver and bacon, a friend from New York, who I did not know was in town, asked if he could join me for coffee.

After exchanging pleasantries, he asked with apparent concern, ''Are you going to eat *that*?''

''Yes, I'm planning to—that's why I ordered it. Why?''

''It's very high in cholesterol. It will kill you!''

''Oh? I've been having liver and bacon for breakfast or lunch and frequently at dinner for a number of years with no apparent ill effects. And what *is* cholesterol?''

''It's in eggs, liver and bacon, kidneys and all sorts of food. It clogs your veins and arteries—produces high blood pressure and kills you!''

''Never heard of it before—I didn't know that. Thanks for telling me, but I think I'll finish this dish.''

At that time the Army National Guard and the large utility which employed me demanded annual physical examinations, and I had a further checkup by my family physician. Although I did not change my diet, I was concerned about my friend's admonition. So, I asked my examining doctors about cholesterol, and if my apparently high cholesterol diet was harmful.

The result of my questioning six doctors, who did not know each other, may be summarized thus:

(1) "First, let me say that we don't know as much about cholesterol and its effects as we should. Your body needs a certain amount of it and has its own mechanism to eliminate what isn't needed."

(2) "When you ask me about cholesterol, you mean, I believe, is there any clogging your circulatory system? If there is, that is bad, dangerous, produces high blood pressure. But just because you eat foods high in cholesterol does not mean that you have absorbed an excess of it into your blood stream."

(3) I asked an examining doctor if he would please test me for cholesterol. He replied, "No, it's expensive, and I can tell you without a test that your blood stream is not clogged with cholesterol. Your blood pressure is normal, very good, there can't be any cholesterol particles clogging your veins or arteries. Don't worry about it."

(4) Another doctor told me, "If you are worried about excess cholesterol in your blood stream, and you shouldn't be because you show no evidence of it, just take a tablespoon of safflower or corn or soy oil in a salad dressing or separately. That will help eliminate any excess cholesterol."

As in other aspects of diet, we tend to be faddists, to act on impulse and unfounded fears, and on somewhat less than scientific newspaper and magazine articles and random comments heard on the radio, failing to check the facts and to consult a medical or nutrition professional. We even disbelieve our own experience! Most of us have little, if any, knowledge of the function of cholesterol and its effects—and many are badly misinformed on the subject. You may be eliminating foods you need because of the suspected "presence" of cholesterol.

It must be recognized, however, that there *is* a direct relation between elevated cholesterol in the blood stream and an excess of triglycerides resulting from poor metabolism of the cholesterol, and cardiovascular disease, particularly coronary artery disease. And there is considerable evidence that there is inherited tendency to high cholesterol and an excess of triglycerides in the blood stream.

In this connection, an interesting research project right after World War II has not received much publicity because of its obvious effects upon the dairy industry, particularly in this country. It has been known for some years that the Eskimos, who have a large intake of animal fat, have almost no coronary artery disease. It has been established also that the people in the lowlands of Europe—Denmark, Holland, and Belgium—who consume a large amount of *milk, butter,* and *cheese*, have an inordinately high incidence of coronary artery disease fairly early in life. During World War II, when the dairy products were taken away from these countries to supply the German Army, the coronary artery disease rate dropped precipitously and was comparable to any other place in the world. Then, within two years after the end of the war, when the dairy product consumption again resumed its usual level in these countries, the coronary artery disease rate reached the previous high level.

So, if you are, or believe you have reason to be, concerned about the amount and effect of cholesterol in foods you enjoy, and the related effects of excess triglycerides, don't be guided by a friend or an advertisement. Consult your physician. Your fears may well be groundless, or the solution may be quite different from what you imagined.

Vitamins and Minerals

For a number of years I have been taking Vitamin C tablets (ascorbic acid), 200 mg. daily, because I had been advised by a medical student, and had read, that doing so would help prevent common winter colds. I seldom "catch" a cold. And I want to keep it that way. I have not had a cold since I have been taking the Vitamin C tablets. But whether or not to credit the "C" tablets for this, I don't know. Nor, I believe, does anyone else. In any event, they have had no known ill effects on me.

A few years ago, I started taking, and am continuing to take, an all and broad-purpose, high-quality, multivitamin and mineral capsule daily. I did—and do—this for two reasons.

First, it seemed to me that with the current deviation from natural foods—high temperature and pressure cooking, freezing and unfreezing, purification, additives, refined flour and sugar, and what-not in the processing, packaging, and preparation—some of the natural vitamins usually provided by nature might be lost.

Second, my friends were routinely taking all sorts of vitamin and mineral tablets or capsules in large potencies with one or more meals daily. They take Vitamin C in doses from 200 mg. to 1,000 mg.; E, B-Complex, B-12, iron, zinc, dolomite, and a variety of combinations of these.

I believe that if you take daily one capsule which combines about twice the recommended daily adult requirement of all the essential vitamins and minerals, that this will reasonably fortify the nutrition provided by a well-balanced diet and that it will be healthier (and easier and less expensive) than taking a number of the included ingredients separately and in larger quantities.

During a routine physical examination I asked my doctor's opinion about taking an all-purpose multivitamin and mineral "pill" daily. His response: "You indicate no vitamin deficiency, so I can hardly prescribe that you take *any* vitamin supplement. But, if it makes you feel better to spend a dime a day for a vitamin pill, why go ahead, it will do you no harm."

Such a high potency multivitamin and mineral capsule is available at most drugstores under a variety of names, and at remarkably different prices for precisely the same formula. The ingredients of these combinations and the quantity of each, based on what is printed on their labels, are:

Vitamins

A	10,000 I.U.
B-1 (thiamine)	10 mg.
B-2 (riboflavin)	10 mg.
B-6 (pyridoxine)	5 mg.
B-12 (cyanocobalamin)	5 mcg.
C	200 mg.

D	400 I.U.
E	15 I.U.
Niacinamide	100 mg.
Calcium Pantothenate	20 mg.

Minerals

Iron	12 mg.
Copper	2 mg.
Magnesium	.65 mg.
Manganese	1 mg.
Zinc	1.5 mg.
Iodine	.15 mg.

Taking vitamin and mineral supplements is a great fad today and the production and marketing of them is a multibillion dollar business. Medical columnists frequently comment on the need for and use of vitamins and minerals, and there is a respectable library of books on the subject.

Conversations with druggists indicate that, like my friends, most people forty years of age and older take a variety of vitamin and/or mineral capsules and tablets daily. Some, relatively few, take just one of the all-purpose, multi-ingredient ("one-a-day") variety. Most take separately—and often in addition to the "multi" type—two to five single vitamin and mineral tablets (C, B-Complex, B-12, E, iron, zinc, as previously noted). Many, unhappily, attempt not only to supplement, but to *correct* faulty diets with bottled vitamins and minerals. This, obviously, is a poor and often dangerous procedure.

Let us now look at some of the features of vitamins—which to an extent applies also to the trace minerals.

First, there is a lot still to be known about the need for and the effects of vitamin intake on the human body and its healthy functioning. And, conversely, there is a great deal of widespread misinformation on the subject as well as a lack of valid scientific evidence based on research, testing, and controlled experimentation. Perhaps least is known about the benefits of Vitamin E from which all sorts of wonders—from growing hair to increasing the sex urge—are expected.

The normal daily requirements of each of the vitamins and minerals has not yet been determined accurately or reliably.

The natural foods we eat, or can and should eat, contain all of the needed vitamins and trace minerals in adequate quantities for good health.

Commercially manufactured vitamin and mineral supplements are generally distributed in units many times the normal daily requirements.

While the body routinely eliminates any excess (unneeded) quantities of most vitamins and minerals, ingesting excessive amounts of some is dangerous. Among the latter are Vitamins A and D.

Some vitamins may counteract the beneficial effects of others.

Although I have been unable to learn of scientific proof of this, it does seem reasonable to believe that continued dependence on vitamin and mineral supplements might well decrease the body's natural and normal process of deriving and using needed vitamins and minerals from the food we eat. It is well known that the use of artificial supports and aids weakens, rather than strengthens, the muscles to which they are applied.

If you take, or plan to take, vitamin and mineral supplements, there are certain basic facts you should know about them.

(1) What are the beneficial effects of each of the commercially prepared vitamins and minerals on your organs and bodily functions?
(2) What ill effects might they have if used in excess of requirements?
(3) Which vitamins and minerals are found in which foods?
(4) What daily quantities of the several vitamins and minerals are recommended by the Food and Nutrition Board, National Research Council, in normal situations?
(5) Do you need vitamin (or mineral) supplements? And if so, which in what quantities?

A final caution. It would seem advisable, before embarking on a program of vitamin and mineral supplements, to review your diet, exercise schedule, and normal daily activity with your doctor and let him suggest what, if any, vitamin and mineral supplement you should, or could, take.

Hair

The hair on your head does not strictly fall in the area of physical fitness. It is included here, however, because in a following section daily massaging of the scalp is one of the procedures suggested for preserving good health. Cosmetic considerations of your hair are included in a following chapter "Your Appearance."

Male pattern baldness and some recession and thinning of the hair in women, as well as men, is difficult to cope with. It is natural; the cells are dead. Also, balding is to an extent hereditary. Daily loss and replacement of *some* hair is normal. You can, however, maintain what hair nature has left on your head in a healthy condition by keeping the scalp clean and helping nature's natural preservation and growth functions by increasing the flow of blood to the scalp by massage.

Lie across your bed with your head unsupported and hanging down over the side. Or, less comfortably, bend over with your head down. With the fingers of both hands, massage the *scalp*; the sides, crown, behind the forehead, for about a minute. Now grasp the nape of your neck below the hairline between your fingers and thumb with your left hand and the width of your forehead below the hairline between the fingers and thumb of your right hand and squeeze and release both areas at the same time while you count twenty slowly.

Then run the small width of a comb vigorously back and forth through all of your hair, followed by the same treatment with a stiff brush. You will feel a pleasant tingling warmth in your scalp.

Do this daily before combing and brushing your hair for the day.

Don't use hair "dressings," oils, lotions and such well-advertised helps to good grooming. They collect dirt, clog pores and interfere with natural hair growth.

Of course, if you have a scalp ailment and undue loss of hair in a short time, see your doctor or a dermatologist immediately.

Some vitamins are said to increase or, in any event, stimulate—the growth of hair. No doubt the lack of normally needed vitamins and minerals in one's diet may affect the growth and health of one's hair. It is dubious, on the other hand, that additional quantities of certain vitamins and minerals (taken internally) will be helpful. Consult your doctor about this.

Teeth

That healthy properly functioning teeth are essential to a healthy body is well known. That we Americans have a high incidence of tooth decay, gum disease, and dental problems is also well recognized. Fortunately, we have a large number of very competent dentists and dental surgeons to correct our dental problems, and a generally reasonable awareness of the total situation.

Good teeth (natural or artificial), clean, of good color, well shaped, properly spaced, have a basic cosmetic value. Good looking teeth, and it is difficult not to expose them in company, are a very important element of good appearance.

The chief cause of the dental decay of natural teeth is the large amount of unrefined sugar we eat. The chief cause of discolored teeth is smoking tobacco.

Retired people seldom have a mouthful of natural teeth. Many have none. The remainder have varying degrees of some. In any case, dental hygiene, care of the teeth (again natural and artificial), is important to good health and good appearance and to inoffensive breath.

The basis of good dental care is simply keeping teeth and dentures clean, and that means cleaning them after *each* meal, as soon as practicable. Keeping teeth clean consists of three, again simple and brief, procedures: 1) ''swishing'' one's mouth with warm water; a little salt or mouthwash lotion added will increase effectiveness; 2) using a medium stiff brush, from the gums toward the teeth; 3) for natural teeth, using dental floss to clean between them.

Most important in the care of your teeth is, of course, regular visits to your dentist—once each six months for a checkup and treatment—and meticulously following his directions.

Simple Daily Good Health Habits

Drink a glass of water first thing in the morning, before each meal and before going to bed. Drink from any water fountain you may pass.

Walk briskly a mile a day, regardless of any other exercise.

Three times a day, take three really deep (diaphragm) breaths—in as unpolluted air as you can find.

Include a bowl of "natural" cereal in your breakfast, along with fruit or fruit juice, and eat a "big" breakfast.

"Swish" your mouth and brush your teeth after each meal.

When you are driving and walking, exercise your eyes by looking well ahead and then down at the closest object nearby, followed by looking far to the left and then the right (without moving your head).

Massage your scalp before you comb and brush your hair in the morning and before going to bed.

When you sit, sit well back in the chair with your back straight along the back of it; do not "lounge" or "sit on your back." From time to time when you are standing, brace three times.

Look ahead and keep your chin up; don't look down unless it is necessary.

Concentrate fully on what you are doing.

7 *Keeping Mentally Alert*

Keeping mentally alert requires frequent and continuing exercise of your mind's primary function, thinking.

You can, on your own initiative, think about what you see, hear, read, and experience—see what you look at. And you can inject yourself into situations which require you to think. Such range all the way from doing a crossword puzzle, through writing simple notes, up to the varied and ever-present problems of managing a small business or successfully operating a small farm.

It is important to remember, also, that a keen, active, and alert mind depends upon a healthy, and therefore active, body. Keeping mentally fit is associated closely with keeping physically fit. Beneficial food, vitamins and minerals, good circulation and fresh oxygen are as important to a good mind as they are to a strong and healthy body.

It is our habit these days to spend a great deal of our spare time (and retirees have a surfeit of that) listening to the radio, watching television, reading newspapers (and more of the comic strips than editorials!), magazines, and books, at moving picture theatres, and at luncheons, dinners, church, and political meetings, listening to speeches. Our intake of knowledge, comment, and entertainment is great indeed but our output, with few exceptions, is minimal. We listen without hearing, we look without seeing, we are told without understanding. We need to *think* about what we see, what we hear, what we are told, and come to a concurrence or disagreement. And we should express these thoughts either verbally or in writing. Unhappily, discussion and debate are becoming lost skills, and lost pleasures.

The challenge of keeping mentally alert is then to make conscious efforts to exercise, to use, your mind. This, in itself, requires thinking and planning. It requires also, and obviously, a good deal of self-discipline.

So what do you do to keep the mental wheels turning and well lubricated—to keep them going instead of rusting? There are many things. For convenience, they may be divided into six broad groupings.

Critical Listening and Viewing

When someone talks with you, when you listen to a sermon, a speech, news and comment on the radio and TV screen, when you are at a play, a movie, reading a book, magazine, an editorial—think about what you have heard and seen and make a summary and then a judgment. You may agree or disagree wholly or, more usually, you will agree and disagree in part. And there are always opportunities for analysis and comparison.

Most important, express your views—in agreement or disagreement—to a companion and, where it is feasible, to the speaker. Where your views are strongly in favor of or opposed to what you have heard or read and it is an important issue, you can, and should, write to the author or to the editor of your local newspaper expressing your views.

How often you hear a companion say, "Wasn't that a great sermon?" and "What a fine speech that was!" If you should reply with, "Yes, it was, what did he say?" you will be met with confusion, embarrassment, and an inaccurate, if any, summary of what the speaker said. The enthusiast heard, but did not listen; did not concentrate on and think about what he heard.

In this context and conversely, it behooves us to think about what we are going to say *before* we express ourselves. This is stimulated by asking, "Is what I am about to say or write relevant to the subject and is it meaningful?"

Verbal Expression

Useful and attractive verbal expression, as is the case in so many other things, requires thought and practice. And practice requires opportunity to do so.

While being a good listener is the essence of good manners and the key to winning friends and being liked, it is also important in view of the same values and in order to exercise your mind to be a good talker and speaker. This means responding, but only *after* listening, and briefly, not talking too much. It means, too, that at the appropriate occasion and time, you will contribute to the conversation or discussion or "question period" with brief, thoughtful, and factual replies and comments.

When you have the opportunity (and often the responsibility) of initiating a conversation or discussion, *think* about what you are going to say. It should, for starters, be of general interest, appealing, timely, brief, and encourage response. This kind of thinking is not easily come by; it requires practice. It is, however, very rewarding.

A very effective and interesting way to practice and enjoy thinking and expressing yourself verbally is to join or start a discussion group. Such a group should not exceed ten members since a greater number precludes discussion, or at least limits it.

Generally, the chairmanship is rotated with that member introducing a subject for discussion. In order to stimulate thinking and full participation the subject should be broad, within the knowledge, experience, and easy comprehension of the members (not technical or specialized) and, to the extent practicable, provocative. Interest and participation will increase if the subject tends toward the philosophic and conceptual rather than the factual and familiar.

Meetings of a discussion group are scheduled most effectively every two weeks with "breaks" during the summer and during the Christmas holidays. A breakfast meeting, as opposed to lunch or dinner, is good since there are fewer conflicts and it provides relief from the usual experience of being *talked to* by a prominent speaker at lunch and dinner meetings.

Writing

Expressing your thoughts and reflections in writing is an excellent means of exercising your mind. You may talk long and forcefully without thinking much (or at all) about what you are saying (as so many so often do), but it is hard to *write* without thinking.

Writing is difficult indeed. But it is not as difficult as you might think it is. It requires only practice, development of the habit, some budgeting of one's time, and *the will to do it*—again, self-discipline.

I am not suggesting that you write a book or magazine article for publication. If, however, you have the capability of doing so, go ahead; it will exercise your mind to the utmost and, at the same time, provide a high degree of personal satisfaction, some financial reward, and a degree of public acclaim. And it is a good test of your ability.

I am suggesting, however, that you set down on paper descriptive reports of and your thoughts about meetings, trips, visits, and amusing or disturbing observations and experiences; that when the occasion, your knowledge, experience, and views permit, you express them in a letter to the editor (previously mentioned in this chapter); that you express (in writing) your views to your elected representatives; that you write to relatives and friends at regular intervals; that you summarize your thoughts, conclusions, objectives, and accomplishments in diary-like notes. Such efforts are interesting exercises, keep you usefully occupied, and, eventually, afford a good measure of pleasure and satisfaction.

Composing rhymes and blank verse is especially challenging and personally rewarding. With practice and study you will develop a reasonable skill in this art form. At worst, it will increase your appreciation of others' published poetry; at best, your poetry will be published.

After you have developed some skill through writing regularly and, again, studying a little, you may well want to try your hand at writing a short story, magazine article or book about your occupation, hobby, experiences, or adventures (during one of our wars, for an example). And, again, you might find an interested publisher.

Fundamentally, however, writing provides the greatest reward in meeting the challenge, in the effort, and in the satisfaction of solid achievement.

Study

Another excellent way to keep your mind active, alert, interested, and usefully occupied is to study. The subject may be a new one or an update on a subject you studied in your school days. It might be academic (history, philosophy, economics, literature) or it might be practical (accounting, business law, surveying, advertising, public relations).

You may want to take a course in your chosen subject through an extension or correspondence school, at a community college, or at a nearby university. All of these present the advantage of compulsion and regularity and of objective testing, appraisal, and grading. Where the time available to you for study, your temperament, ability as a student, knowledge, and experience combine to make it desirable and feasible to set your own study schedule and objectives, this is a sound course to pursue. The necessary books and forms can be purchased or borrowed from a college or public library.

Apart from the academic and vocational type courses, you can set up for yourself a course of study of the Bible, the dictionary (ten new words a day—what you think they mean and what they do mean), a reading of the preface, introductory matter, and the appendixes of the dictionary, *Bartlett's Familiar Quotations,*

Roget's Thesaurus, and a book of synonyms and antonyms.

Researching the history of your community and your family and studying the lives of distinguished men and women and battles and wars can be both interesting and fruitful and provide an unusual challenge. (Are you a Civil War or World War I or II buff perhaps?)

Learning to speak a foreign language through close association with neighbors and friends who migrated here after their youth and are now bilingual presents an especially interesting and pleasant means of acquiring a new skill and some knowledge of another culture.

Games and Puzzles

There are many mentally stimulating games which cause you to think, study, concentrate, remember, and imagine. Several involve playing cards, others are puzzles, questions and answers, and games played on boards with figures.

At the top of the list of mind-twisters is probably chess. At a lower level of challenge are backgammon, checkers, dominoes, mah jong; the card games—bridge, cribbage, gin rummy, poker, solitaire, and a host of others (see Hoyle!); crossword and jigsaw puzzles and other such; true-false, multiple choice, and other question and answer games and tests. There are, of course, many more than I have mentioned.

The important thing about mental games, puzzles, and tests is to play or do one or more of them regularly—for fun and for mental exercise. Play backgammon with your spouse every other evening or chess with a companion twice a week; play rubber or duplicate bridge two or three times a week and do the crossword puzzle in your newspaper daily, or do whatever pleases and challenges you most. But, whatever that is, do it regularly, keep at it, and stay with it.

Planning and Setting Objectives

In retirement you do not have much need to plan, and what there is is seldom urgent. There is even less need to set objectives.

However, planning for the near and farther-off future (and setting measurable objectives and achieving them) is a very satisfying mental exercise. It develops assurance and confidence, and is often rewarding. Since the end result of planning and setting objectives is achievement, and since achievement itself is a highly exhilarating experience and admired by others, it follows that the preliminary planning and establishing of objectives is also stimulating.

As one of several means of keeping your mind active and alert, it is well to develop these procedures (planning and setting objectives) as a habit. Many day-to-day activities lend themselves to it. Some are: your daily, weekly, and monthly expense budget; your exercise program; your reading, writing, and study projects; visits to friends and relatives; maintenance and replacement needs inside and outside the house; disposition of unused possessions; personal weight reduction; visiting places of interest in your city or community which you have taken for granted and neglected. With these as a foundation, others will suggest themselves. This subject (Planning and Setting Objectives) is covered again, in more detail, under "Achievement" in the chapter "Remaining Active."

There are a number of ways to remain mentally alert. It requires only doing what it takes—and the will to do that.

8   Remaining Active

General

Many doctors, physical fitness experts, gerontologists, and social researchers have discovered that inactivity is a major cause of aging and, therefore, untimely death. By the same token, remaining active is perhaps the greatest assurance of a long and interesting life.

Broadly, the exertion of mental or physical energy might qualify as being active. Reading, watching TV, looking at a ball game, going to the movies, maybe even "touring" in an automobile should perhaps be included in being active. In a way they are properly so classified and, in another way, they should not be.

More correctly, it seems being active needs to include serious purpose and a specific objective, a goal—output rather than intake. There needs to be stimulation and challenge and effort. You have to put out to be actively active.

Active activity will generally fall into one or all of these five categories: mental, physical, organizational, social, and travel and exploration.

Mental activity would include solving problems, making decisions, planning, organizing, study, research, analysis, writing, and other such efforts. This is covered in the preceding chapter "Keeping Mentally Alert."

Physical active activity would include (1) "working"— farming, gardening, planting; breeding, raising, fattening and marketing cattle, sheep, horses; building and painting; and the like, and (2) exercise, sports and athletic games—golf, tennis, fishing, skating, skiing, swimming, sailing, cycling, jogging, horseback riding, walking several miles vigorously, and such. Much of this is covered in the preceding chapter "Keeping Physically Fit."

Organizational activities would include serious and responsible involvement in civic, church, political, educational, recreational, development and similar organizations.

Social activities include visiting family and friends, visits from family and friends; cocktail, breakfast, lunch, dinner, and supper parties; dances; weddings; bridge, poker and bingo parties; and a host of other functions designed to bring together friends, neighbors, and others with a common interest.

Travel and exploration would seem to require no definition.

The important thing is that your activity, or activities, be related to definite objectives against which you can measure accomplishment.

If you are engaged in planning, organizing, study, research, or analysis, you will almost necessarily set task and time objectives —intermediate and final.

In the area of physical activity, whether work, exercise, or sport, reward and satisfaction will be increased if you set your effort against a progressive standard of accomplishment and time.

Setting specific tasks and achievement objectives, and a time within which to accomplish them, will make the responsibilities you have undertaken in organizational activities a great deal more interesting, rewarding, and satisfying than they would be otherwise.

Travel and exploration would, by their very nature, require specific objectives with respect to cost, purpose, place, and time.

Other than the necessary planning of the events themselves— and this is usually a sizeable task requiring considerable talent— social events would appear properly to be a relaxation from other activities. Creative art (painting, sculpture, music, ballet, writing, sophisticated photography, metal design, wood carving, cabinet making) is highly rewarding in terms of achievement, as is a serious and knowledgeable devotion to collecting books, stamps and coins, shells, and whatnot.

An occasional relaxation from concentration on more serious pursuits, puttering in the garden, spending a longer time than usual in front of the TV screen, reading light literature, being a spectator in the sports arena, viewing indifferent to poor movies, and other such aspects of loafing are, to an extent, therapeutic. But, in this connection, it is important to remember that there is no such thing as a permanent vacation. A vacation derives its value and its meaning by being a relief or change from and an interruption to, a regular occupation. If you *were* on a "permanent" vacation, you would benefit by and perhaps need relief from its sameness and boredom by "working" or engaging in some other form of compulsory activity for a while.

Some of the foregoing thought is illustrated in a seemingly unrelated incident. A friend asked a horse show judge at the end of a very long day alone in the ring if he wasn't thoroughly bored as well as tired from watching so many horses—and often the same ones—doing essentially the same thing for so long a time.

"Perhaps I should be," the judge replied, "but really I'm not either bored or tired. As a matter of fact I enjoyed the day. There were some very good performances, some excellent rides, and some of the poor ones were interesting because they need not have been so poor. You see, I have to concentrate on and appraise each horse that comes into the ring, and make a decision at the end of each class. This is absorbing and challenging—so I'm quite unaware of the passage of time!"

Permit me now to inject a few case histories:

Consider my good friend John S. He was before and for some eight years after his retirement a talented writer, news analyst, and expert in the public relations field. He had two immediate retirement projects. One was a modest horse farm and the other, to work on the book he had always wanted to write. He accepted invitations to membership in two distinguished discussion groups as well as several civic clubs and community associations. His exercise included riding his horse, playing golf, and walking and swimming. He liked good food and had a tendency to be over-weight, but he controlled it. Surely his was a good retirement program. That is, it would have been, had he stayed with it. He did not.

My friend John let his resolve and his activities slip. He abandoned his purpose. He began to take it easy. Occasionally he would let slip an "I'm too old for that," "at my age you know...."

John read more and more, listened attentively at meetings, listened to the radio, and watched his TV screen. And John wrote seldom, discussed little, found an increasing number of excuses for not exercising, sold his good riding horse, and played only nine holes of golf on foot at each outing—then rode a cart. His paunch became more pronounced, his shoulders more stooped; he had difficulty rising out of a soft chair and sofa and his stride shortened, slowed, and lost its spring; his speech became some-what hesitant.

John was not ill, but suddenly he was getting old—rusting out.

Then there was Bill H., active and successful head of a large corporation. He retired voluntarily at age sixty-two with a substantial income and attractive stock options. He was, in his words, "through with business and finance. I'm going to take it easy, loaf, do the leisure type of things I never had time to do. Yes sir, I'm going to enjoy my well-earned retirement."

Bill did just that. He fished, played golf, went to practically every cocktail and dinner party to which he and his wife were invited, spent the summers on "the cape" and winters in Florida, cruising the Mediterranean or visiting "the islands." He spent a lot of time in the taproom of his club "having one with the boys."

Bill gave generously to his church, many charitable and civic organizations, his political party. But he would not accept any of the offers and appeals for active membership as an officer, committee member, vestryman, or to teach a course at the community college or conduct a seminar.

Bill was, indeed, having fun as he saw it. But Bill was becoming a pretty dull fellow, as uninteresting as he was disinterested, becoming as pudgy in mind as he was in body.

A mutual friend commented to me, "Bill is pretty boring. His stories, jokes, and comments are not very good and he repeats them too often. Did you tell me that he was president of XYZ?"

"Yes, he was—and not many years ago."

"That's hard for me to believe. He must have been able and alert to hold that job, but he sure has slipped a lot since then. Too bad!"

I had a great horse some years ago in the days of the horse cavalry. Marse Henry by chronological age only was old, twenty-three—nearly 100 in equivalent human age. He carried me safely, swiftly, and enjoyably in pursuit of the fox in the fall and won ribbons, largely blue ones, in small and medium shows in hunter, jumper, and hack classes throughout the year. During the summer of his twenty-third year, we won three "Cavalry Field Tests." These required negotiating approximately eighteen miles of all manner of natural country and some twenty-four natural and constructed obstacles ("jumps"), and were decided on time, condition and jumping.

Marse Henry looked and acted and performed like a horse less than half his age. Except for the few who knew, no one would believe he was as old as I said he was. And those who knew his age had trouble believing what he did. At one of the field tests an officer said to me as we were about to start, "Is that Marse Henry you're riding?"

"Yes, it is," I replied, "and I'll bet you five dollars he wins!"

"Wins?" said my friend, "Why he'll never finish!"

"A hundred on that," I replied.

He accepted the five dollars to win bet—and lost.

What was the secret of Marse Henry's youth, health, and success? I worked him a hard two hours or more nearly every day.

When I went off to the war, a friend offered to keep him for me. I was delighted and cautioned him to keep working Marse Henry—that this was what kept him young.

A year and a half later my friend wrote to me, overseas, to tell me that Marse Henry had lost so much condition he had to have him "put down."

I asked, in my return letter, "Did you work him nearly every day as I requested?" His reply was, "No, he was too old for regular hard work."

My mental response, "So you thought you were being kind to him—but you killed him."

To return to the basic theme, mere observation and concentration provide something, but not much, or at least not enough. To obtain real benefit from an experience you have to participate actively, even if it is only discussion, review, analysis, summary, study, comparison, decision.

Perhaps it is fair to say that to be truly active you can't just take in—you have to put out!

Because you have time to give while others are "working," and because over the years before retirement you have developed both specific skills and knowledge and the wisdom and judgement that come from experience, you have a lot to offer. And there are many who will be glad to use those qualities in a variety of meaningful occupations.

Let us now consider some specific activities to remain active.

Civic Activities

All kinds of organizations, broadly grouped under the title of civic endeavors, are more than happy to have retired people join in their good works for the benefit of the community. They will welcome you and, as a matter of fact, they *need* your help.

Nearly all civic organizations rely heavily on volunteer officers and workers. Retired people have the time, ability, and experience to fill key positions and handle important jobs, and with a minimum of conflicting interests. Involvement in civic activities provides not only an interesting, pleasing, and challenging occupation, but also the satisfaction which comes from serving your fellow men.

The range of civic activities is large. Some are:

Business Service Clubs: Rotary, Kiwanis, Lions, Chamber of Commerce, Junior Chamber of Commerce, Ruritan, Civitan.

Historical, Development, Planning commissions and associations.

Taxpayers, Area Improvement and Protective associations.

Relief Organizations: the American National Red Cross, the local rescue squad, the volunteer fire department in your community, Recording for the Blind, hospital auxiliaries.

Youth Groups: Boy and Girl Scouts, 4-H projects, Future Farmers of America (FFA) and others.

Community Projects to help the underpriviledged and handicapped. There are a host of these, ranging from day nurseries for migratory workers' children and cultural and intellectual centers in the ghettos, to neighborhood vegetable gardens and adult education.

If there are none of these types of projects in your community, you have the challenging opportunity to *start* one.

Animal Protective Societies: the Society for the Prevention of Cruelty to Animals (SPCA), various "shelters," protection of endangered species and others.

Veterans Organizations: If you are a veteran of one of our nation's several wars, there are some ten or more major organizations you can join and in which you can become active.

Fraternal Organizations: Free Masons, Odd Fellows, BPOE, Loyal Order of the Moose, and many others.

Additionally, there is a surprising number of special interest and special qualification organizations which might have appeal—Knights of Columbus; the SAR, SR, and DAR; the Audubon Society; St. Andrews, St. Georges, the Knickerbocker and such societies; the Society of the Cincinnati; and so on through a long list.

It is evident that there is ample opportunity for large and even full involvement in a number of fields in the area of civic activity. All that you need to do is select an organization and the type of work for which you are qualified and which you enjoy, and tell the head of the organization you select (or its secretary) that you are able, willing, and ready to take on a job. More likely, you won't have to do this. *They* will be looking for *you* and *invite* you to join them!

In your local library you will find a number of reference books listing all sorts of organizations which welcome volunteers and some, usually government funded, which offer a modest stipend. From among those lists you should be able to select several which suit your abilities and desires.

Your local or nearby RSVP (Retired Senior Volunteer Program) organization has as its specific objective the placement of volunteers over sixty. You might find contacting that organization helpful.

Church Activities

There is hardly an area where the assistance of able and energetic men and women is more needed and more appreciated than in church work. Certainly involvement in this field should provide special satisfaction.

A large proportion of the lay responsibility and activity of churches is discharged by women because, no doubt, male members of the church are largely employed or managing their own businesses.

It follows then that retired men are much in demand to help with the work of their churches—in the vestry or other governing bodies, to head and serve on committees, to guide youth groups, and so on. And such help is much appreciated.

People move about a great deal more today than they did fifty to sixty years ago, and individuals find, as a result of this and along with other reasons, little real identity with the community. Church attendance is falling off or increasing very slowly. In addition, opportunities for recreational activity have increased vastly in the last twenty-five years, and many seem to prefer motoring to the country, visiting out of town, and playing golf or tennis to attending church. To place the church in proper perspective with respect to these diversions is challenging and necessary.

The church is changing and trying to put itself more in tune with the times. Many have planning committees, research groups, and similar setups which require a reasonably sophisticated and experienced membership.

Former business and professional men can make an especially meaningful contribution to these new requirements in church life with compensating challenge and reward.

Social Life

Parties (luncheon, cocktail, dinner, supper, and sometimes breakfast) provide one of the basic elements of our social structure. And they cover a wide range of interest and enjoyment. They are indeed pleasant, but, in general, they are the least productive and healthy of our activities.

While conversation can be gay and discussion stimulating, you cannot always remain in the company of the bright ones nor get away from the dull. One thing is certain though, drink is ample and the food is rich (both are fattening), inhalation of smoke and still air is unavoidable, the noise level is high, the heat above normal, and everyone, in his and her way, has fun.

No, I am not at all "against" parties; I believe that I enjoy them more than most. I wish only to emphasize that in retirement you have the opportunity and the privilege to control party going more than the young and the employed. These are motivated and, to a degree, controlled in their social activities by ambition, and frequently some insecurity; by the desire or necessity of making an impression, seizing an opportunity, and other factors of this nature.

In retirement you are (or should be) released from such bonds. You are not "running for office." There is no one you need impress (it is you who are impressive). You have most of the honors you will get. You know whom you like and whom you do not; since you have "arrived," you have no social ambition.

The point is that you need only attend those social functions that please you—those that seem worthwhile. It is unnecessary and it seems silly to waste time on any others. The other consideration is that to spend a great deal of time, even at social functions you enjoy, would seem to interfere materially with any serious pursuit and with more rewarding and challenging uses of your valuable time.

A periodic examination and appraisal of your social activities might prove beneficial. And it might be especially profitable to determine whether you are seeing enough of the people you like and perhaps too much of people in whom you have only a passing interest but to whom you feel you are socially obligated (avoiding this in itself takes some foresight, planning, and courage). If so, then chart a new course. You owe this to yourself and you can afford it!

Reading

We read for pleasure and recreation (to keep in touch and *au courant*) and knowledge (as opposed to information), and for most of us the reasons are in the order noted. The amount of time spent in reading varies, as a rule, with one's interest, the number of books, periodicals, and newspapers readily available, the amount of time which may be used for this purpose, competition of the radio and the TV screen, and one's temperament.

Nearly everyone reads one or more newspapers daily—the local paper and often, in addition, one published in a nearby city or the "New York Times," the "Washington Post," or the "Wall Street Journal." Almost everyone also subscribes to, or has delivered, a weekly or monthly news review and summary type magazine, "Reader's Digest," and one or more "trade" journals—those devoted to furniture building, garden and flower care, sailing, automobiles, and whatnot. Then there are the alumnus (and alumnae) periodicals, the company house organs, annual reports, children's and grandchildren's school publications, military and veteran's organization newsletters—and "junk" mail in large quantities.

Anyway, there are many, too many, periodicals to read. And most of them are not read. So there is precious little, if any, time left to read a book or study the contents of textbooks.

If you are active in your retirement, you will have no more time for reading than you did prior to retirement. In contrast to the situation prior to retirement, however, you will be in a position to *plan* to devote as much time to reading (and *what* to read) as you wish. And here is the key to purposeful and productive occupation of the time devoted to reading—planning.

Your plan for reading might include (1) the objective of your reading; (2) what you intend to read; (3) the source of your reading material; (4) the amount of time to be devoted to this activity; and (5) the specific time and days of the week to be set aside for it. This does not mean that you will not and should not occasionally read just for the fun of it—without plan, rhyme, or reason. But this is a diversion and relaxation from the main theme of useful purposeful occupation, which again, is the theme of an *active* retirement.

There are many attractive purposes in reading—an expanded knowledge of history, geography, astronomy and space science (pertinent today), literature itself, a broadening of general background through pursuing a course of reading in an encyclopaedia, the "Five Foot Bookshelf" or something similar, and others.

Another worthwhile project is to reread the classics (especially the backbone of all of them, Shakespeare and the Bible) and other books which impressed you during your school and college days. You may find it rewarding too, to reread some tongue in cheek books, like *Alice in Wonderland*, whose serious purpose and philosophic content is seldom recognized or appreciated by the young. There are other authors—Washington Irving, Emerson, Thoreau, Mark Twain, O. Henry, Bret Harte, Dick Davis, Rudyard Kipling, James Branch Cabell—who may remain unappreciated without a rereading. And the fables of Aesop and some of the fairy tales can be reread with profit, interest, and entertainment.

You might find it both interesting and challenging to reflect on which five books you would like for company if you ran out of fuel over a bountiful, uninhabited, and remote semitropical island in your single-seated jet. After you have decided (and coming to the decision will provide a lively topic of conversation) read and reread the five books you selected.

A reading of books about and relative to your local area and books by local authors is bound to be satisfying—if only through personal identity.

A possibly interesting adventure in reading is to stop in at the college (if there is one near you) or high school bookshop to find out what the young are reading and dip into their literature. And related to this, you might study the best-seller list to see how up to date you are. If you find you are not "with it," perhaps you can become a little "mod," or, at any rate develop an aquaintance with what's new through the best-seller lists.

Periodicals and newspapers crowd in on you; they are demanding and hard to avoid. A friend commented to me concerning the voluminous Sunday newspapers, that he neither ordered nor read it. "Why?" I asked. "Well, if I have it at home or, for that matter, if it's in front of me anywhere, if I see it—I feel a great compulsion, a sort of duty to read it; all of it. That takes a long time, and I haven't that much time for that purpose!"

It is very difficult to do, but a careful, thoughtful, and honest review of the magazines and newspapers to which you subscribe and receive through other means (with a view to examining critically their value to you), will pay substantial dividends. Among them are good use of your time and avoiding the harassment caused by believing you *must* read all you receive. Such a review might, indeed, result in *increasing* your reading material. More likely by far, however, it will indicate that you should *reduce* the number of magazines and papers you are confronted with.

Some enjoy displaying on a living room, library, or study table a number of prestigious magazines. This is fine and presents no problem, provided the old magazines are thrown or given away as soon as the new issues arrive.

If the time budgeted for reading is not enough to read all of the magazines and papers you feel that you should, you might quickly look through them, confining yourself largely to headlines, tables of contents, the headings of articles, and chapter headings, and cut or tear out the material you would like to read but can't get around to at the time. This procedure will reduce the bulk and accelerate both reading and final disposal.

Frequently we find ourselves waiting for people with whom we have an engagement, at functions, for transportation, for a meal to be served, and other instances where the time set or expected is not met. Since an active person in, as well as prior to, retirement never has time to kill, but only to use, it is helpful always to carry something to read with you. This might be one or another of the clipped or torn-out pages previously referred to, a magazine, a paperback book, or even a small hard-covered one. In this way, waiting time can be used profitably—and irritability with the need for waiting is reduced or even eliminated.

In summary, reading can be both fun and effective (and useful and stimulating) if you (1) develop a *purpose* with respect to it; (2) thoughtfully *select* your reading material; and (3) *budget* your reading time.

On the subject of reading, however, a caution.

Reading is an *intake* process—a valuable and useful one indeed, as set forth in the preceding paragraphs. But essential to being active is *putting out*. Except when you read only for relaxation and recreation, you must not sit in a chair for long periods and *just* read. You need to *do* something with and about what you have read. You need to think about it, discuss it, make notes, write about it; digest, develop and use what you have read! And use at least some of it as a stimulation to action, to output!

Writing

Nearly everyone believes that he has in him or her the makings of a great novel—if only he could find the time to get at it. The itch to write seems even greater than the itch to paint. Most of us, when we finish reading a good story or a well done article wonder why *we* didn't write it. It seems so easy. But it isn't.

The rewards for good writing are great. It is a considerable satisfaction just to express your thoughts; it is greater if what you have written appears in any manner of public print and, presumably, is appreciated by others; it is great if what you write is recognized by a check—and greatest if it is a substantial one. And, of course, it is among the greater thrills to see your name on a book or at the head of an article in a magazine or newspaper.

Writing is indeed rewarding. But success, satisfaction, recognition, and reward, given a reasonable ability, is in direct proportion to study and practice. Actually, the only way to learn to write is to write.

If you want to enjoy the deep satisfaction of seeing your name on the cover of a book or at the head of a magazine article, and the material reward that goes with it, you need to study and to work hard. You can do this by setting yourself a definite work schedule. Write about anything—an experience, a visit, a trip, the appearance of the sky in early morning and late at night, your thoughts, your "athletic" activities, the changing scene at home. Write regularly—every day and for a minimum duration of fifteen minutes. Then, as quickly as you can, work up to writing one, then two hours.

Study to develop skill and competence in writing involves four basic areas:

(1) Enlarged and effective vocabulary—the meaning and use of words.
(2) Grammar—especially sentence structure and punctuation.
(3) Style—includes the use of short and long sentences, economy of words, variety in expression, good paragraphing, and, most important, variations in and modifications of traditional usage. *The Elements of Style* by William Strunk, Jr., and E. B. White is a classic in this area.
(4) Studying the works of successful authors.

You need to learn the distinction between "house" and "home" and how best to use each—whether or not a preposition is a good thing to end a sentence with—which "person" to use—if the active voice should be used always—effective punctuation—when to repeat the same word for emphasis and when to avoid using the same word—the proper way to use question marks and quotations—and so on and so on.

Most important and most effective in influencing both your style and skill is to select the two authors (successful ones, of course) you enjoy most. That is, two whose style, presentation, and subject matter you like especially. Then study carefully how they write. Then write something about a page long, or perhaps two, in what you believe to be the style of one of them. Practice this frequently, attempting to imitate one and then the other.

Several years ago, a magazine for which I did a few articles asked me to condense Kipling's attractive and popular little story called ''The Maltese Cat.'' It is concerned with a polo pony in a polo game in the glorious imperial days of Britain's army in India.

I struggled with what I knew was a very tough assignment for weeks. The best I could do was to eliminate one rather short paragraph, a word here and there and very few sentences, for a total of something less than a page!

Mr. Kipling was a very skilled writer—an experienced craftsman. Every word he used meant so much that it could not be eliminated without destroying or changing the meaning, losing continuity, or damaging his most attractive style.

There are a number of schools which provide instruction through well set up correspondence courses. Most universities and community colleges offer courses in creative writing and English literature on a regular and extension course basis. Through these sources, you should have no difficulty obtaining the instruction and guidance you need.

Writing is indeed particularly rewarding for the time spent on it. But two things determine that. First, a real desire to express your thoughts in writing. Second, a willingness to do the hard work required for success: study, practice, diligence, and concentration.

Study—New Skills

You *can* indeed teach an old dog new tricks—if he is agile and willing to learn. And, certainly, you can teach an older man or woman a new trade, a new technique, to develop a new interest.

Even better, he and she can teach themselves.

After retiring, some sailors become horsemen and some horsemen become sailors; some businessmen become successful storekeepers, wholesalers, warehousemen, and mechanics; men and women who for years have worked at a desk learn to use their hands to great advantage, and men and women who have worked for years with their hands learn to appreciate art, music, and dancing and to enjoy poetry and the prose classics. Many oldsters return to school to finish diploma or degree requirements with marked success.

I recall visiting a retired cavalryman at his attractive new home near an inlet on which his boat floated. With considerable pride, he pointed out that he had lowered the height of the old house one floor and then showed me the several rooms he had altered materially—where he had added a doorway, taken out a wall. He remarked, almost as if it were a daily occurrence, that he had, single-handedly, laid out and laid down the soapstone terrace I had admired. He had also constructed a brick wall and a short brick walk and the dock.

"You were always a good horseman but I never knew you to use a hammer except on a horseshoe nail. Wherever did you learn to be such a master builder and construction worker?" I asked him.

"By hanging around building jobs, observing and asking questions, and by reading easily obtained pamphlets, many published by Uncle Sam and by paint, lumber, and hardware companies. I just got interested, picked up the knowledge and gained some skill by practice, by practical application. Of course I made some mistakes. Fortunately none was very costly and I didn't make the same mistake twice—not often anyway."

My friend's curiosity, observation, self-confidence and determination paid off—literally.

Another Army friend of mine (this one had transferred from the Infantry to the Air Force) had the same viewpoint as my cavalry friend, but it didn't pay off as well. Understandably, in his new assignment he wanted to wear a pilot's wings. He was five years over the age limit for flight training. He pleaded to be permitted at least to take the rigorous physical examination. This, with some difficulty, was arranged. And he passed it. He had flown in the cockpit of various aircraft often enough to remark, "If some of these not overbright young men can fly these airplanes, I am sure that I can." But the regulations held firm; he was not permitted to take flight training. So he took private lessons, did well, passed the necessary civilian tests, and now has a civilian pilot's license and flys rented airplanes.

Another friend of mine retired from a financial post of some responsibility with a large firm. He enjoyed the land, wanted to be out of doors. He decided to study surveying. He took a correspondence course, "audited" some classes at the university in a nearby city, worked indoors and out with a local surveying company, and in due course qualified as a licensed land surveyor.

If you find study and the acquisition of new skills and interests appealing, you may wish to concentrate your efforts in one area. On the other hand, you may find it more satisfying to venture into two or three new fields. If variety appeals to you, a good balance may be achieved by combining an athletic or manual skill with study in an area that primarily requires reading and research or collecting and for analyzing data.

A good vehicle for study in academic and business fields is the extension course programs offered by most universities and community colleges. Chances are good that these courses, designed for adults, are available in your town or in one a short drive away.

It may prove helpful, in choosing a new field of endeavor (or several), to classify the various areas in which you may wish to study, acquire a new or improved skill, or build a new or deeper or broader interest. I suggest the following as being convenient.

Athletic Games and Sports. Golf, tennis (but don't play singles too vigorously!), archery, badminton, swimming, hiking, jogging, curling and skating (where there is ice), sailing, fishing, and a host of other such absorbing, stimulating, and healthy outdoor activities.

Basic Manual Skills. Carpentry, masonry, electrical work, radio and TV repair, automotive design and repair, furniture upholstering.

Crafts and Artistic Skills. Photography, taxidermy, ceramics, silver and iron design, wood carving, cabinet making (full size and miniature), painting, drawing.

Collecting. Stamps, coins, books, maps, battlefield momentos, bookplates, swords, pistols, rifles, antiques, match covers, and whatnot!

Games of Mental Skill. Bridge, chess, backgammon, checkers, and several other such and crossword puzzles. Study, concentration, and practice will make you an expert and a much sought partner and opponent.

Study. Largely for information and general knowledge, flowers, birds, trees (these have the added incentive of taking you outdoors much of the time), investment of funds, financial newspapers, journals and reports, civic organizations, consumer reports, books on space exploration, computer technology, advanced use of calculators.

Study. Academic subjects—economics, philosophy, English, a foreign language, political science, geophysics, geology, geography, astronomy, taxation, business law—any of the courses which appeal to you in the humanities, literature, and languages and the less difficult areas of the sciences and mathematics.

Of all the activities suitable for and suited to the retired, study and the acquisition of new skills would seem to be particularly rewarding and provide special satisfaction in accomplishment, and this activity is apt to last longer than most others. If your study or skill results in accomplishing something creative, the reward and satisfaction is immeasurably increased.

And who knows? You might easily become an expert in your newly chosen field and earn substantial fees for sharing your knowledge and skill with the less well informed and able. If, on the other hand, you realize no financial gain from this source you have, at any rate, the satisfaction of possessing something of great value which no one can take from you.

In this connection, as in some others, it is well to remember that what you save, you may lose; what you spend, you have always!

Travel

Most travel for relaxation and rest; they consider it a vacation and use vacation time for this purpose. About travel as a vacation, as a relaxation from other activity, I have no comment.

However, travel as a major activity of retired people is first subject to the same comments, made previously, about a "permanent" vacation, that there is no such thing. Travel, as a major and continuing activity, needs to have a purpose.

Having a purpose in travel means, in effect, that travel is secondary, incidental; that you have something meaningful to do, a specific project, which, in the doing, requires you to travel.

There are many interesting fields of endeavor which, in their nature, require you to travel in pursuit of your objective. Among them are archeology, collecting antiques, geology, architecture, museums, battlefield momentos, a study of stud farms, rare flora and fauna, photographic safaris, the folkways and mores of the few remaining relatively primitive peoples and, of course, many others of these kinds.

Another interesting basis for travel is a study of the habits, dress, economy, industry, foods and beverages, education, religious practices, folkways and mores, and other characteristics of the people of various foreign lands and continents.

At some point you will want to consider the means of getting to where you need to obtain what you are seeking. You have a choice of ship or airplane if your destination is across the sea, or of motor (car or bus), train, or airplane if your interests require travel in North, South or Central America (although some of the areas in these localities may also be reached by ship). Travel by airplane is fastest, of course, and usually, but not always, the most expensive. Many *enjoy* flying (I among them), although more probably do not. If getting to your destination quickly is the primary consideration, then of course, you will want to fly there. Otherwise, a more leisurely mode of travel is appealing.

If the time to reach your destination is of no serious consequence, and if you are not unduly bothered by rough seas, then travel aboard ship is a real delight and a "vacation" in addition. The days at sea are gay and at the same time restful and healthful. On a per day basis the cost is also very moderate.

Travel in your own car, by bus, and by train is in general less comfortable than by either ship or airplane. There are times and places when and where the scenery is enjoyable. Unhappily, much of an overland trip is necessarily (because of the route) dreary and monotonous. When you are driving, there is opportunity for little save close concentration on the road and the business of driving, and the wear on the human chasis is great. Travel by rail used to be fun. The coaches were clean and comfortable, service was excellent, the food was very good, and the club car provided a gay meeting place. The airplane, private automobile, and long distance bus, and, I suppose, apathy and discouragement on the part of the railroads, have downgraded materially all aspects of travel by train. But, who knows, there may be a resurgent turnabout!

Then there are sentimental journeys near and far—nostalgic places to revisit to recall an occasion and to compare.

With a purposeful approach, your travel will generate much more interest and enjoyment than just "taking a trip" and having a purpose will add lustre to it. In addition, the trip will gain a greater significance as a conversation piece and as a recollection.

Of course, developing a purpose for a trip or trips or taking a trip for a purpose—the manner in which the objective is to be realized, how the results will be summarized, the basis for conclusions, study and preparation—all of these require much thought and planning. This is part of the fun. All of it, plus the exhilaration and novelty and excitement of the "incidental" voyage, makes the whole project satisfying, lasting, rewarding, and valuable.

Exploration

The purpose of some trips might well be simply exploration, the adventure of seeking out the unfamiliar and the unknown—a journey of discovery. Splendid, absorbing and exciting, but also apt to be expensive.

You need not, however, go far from home to enjoy exploration.

For example, if you live in the country, as you motor to town, or as you drive to pay a visit or perform an errand, no doubt you frequently wonder where an obscure side road goes. And you may wonder about the scenic value and comfort of alternate routes, and guess where an unknown road will lead you. Perhaps you have heard of a new development you would like to see, or some new construction. So you resolve that one day you will venture down that road and find out where it does go. But seldom do you do this.

If you live in a big city there are sure to be parts of it you have never visited, some streets you have not heard of, important places you have not seen. Of course you mean to explore them one day.

It is well established and well known that the nearer one lives to a famous landmark, ''sight,'' or location of a celebrated event, the less likely one is to visit it.

A surprisingly small number of the millions who live in New York City and its suburbs have visited Bedloe's Island, on which the Statue of Liberty is located, while hardly a visitor has not; many New Yorkers have never seen their city's Chinatown or the Bowery or visited the New York Stock Exchange or Grant's Tomb, although most visitors have. People taking a holiday in New York find going to the theater and the museums a necessity, while only a small number of New Yorkers enjoy these treats in their midst with any regularity. Why? Because they feel that since these goodies are close at hand, they can take advantage of them at any time they wish. A time that seldom, sometimes never, comes.

In my adopted state of Virginia, so rich in history and natural beauty, there are some twenty outstanding and important places which would provide great reward in cultural and artistic enrichment for the little effort required to visit them. The number of such interesting places could easily be tripled in this fortunate land. And how many residents of the Commonwealth have visited the first-ranked twenty? A rather small and perhaps somewhat biased sample indicates there are few; again, it seems that in exposure to historic shrines and nature's wonders in Virginia the tourists substantially outscore the natives.

I recall a story I heard some years ago. An American traveller admiring the Rhine River from an especially good vantage point turned to a man near him, evidently a German, and remarked on the beauty of the river with great enthusiasm and some awe. His companion, in good English, agreed that it was indeed a wonderful sight, a remarkable gift of nature and then added, "As a matter of fact, in my extensive travels I have found only one other such view which is more appealing."

"Where could that possibly be?" the American inquired, obviously surprised.

"In your country, there's a bend in the Hudson River near Garrison that provides a really breathtaking view."

"Near Garrison?" remarked the American in astonished disbelief. "Why that's where I live!"

To get the most out of your explorations, nearby or far away, you have to plan them. Make your exploration a project. Setting up the project is itself fun.

So, in your active retirement you may wish, along with purposeful travel, to include local exploration as one of your activities. You will find it exciting and interesting to search out (or perhaps just notice) out of the way lanes, country byroads, new and alternate routes. Then note a day and time to explore them. And maybe you will enjoy writing down something about each experience and some thoughts inspired by it. Others may enjoy reading what you write about your explorations; the venture might even be profitable. Some years ago I recall enjoying a book titled *Loafing Down Long Island.*

Then, of course, there are the nearby places of historic interest and nature's wonders which you must see—or see again. So, once more, put local exploration on your list and leave the moon and mountaintops to those a little younger.

Shopping

A couple whom I know well enjoys shopping. They like bargains, they like to get full value (or a little more) for their dollar and for their dime. This despite being financially well-off.

They go from shop to shop to find the one which will sell the same product of the same quality in the same quantity for the lowest price, or for the same price with trading stamps or some other bonus added. This is expensive if you take into account the time and fuel consumed and the wear and tear on the car and the personal chasis, but it's fun. It's an interesting and challenging game. And who doesn't get a kick out of a bargain—even if it only *seems* like one?

Another approach to shopping, which also can be both interesting and challenging, is to become thoroughly familiar with the shops you frequent regularly because of their superior service or convenient location. Here you can learn where in the shop and when bargains can be found, where the things you want or might want are located, what's new, the savings from buying larger quantities, how the prices of packaged foods compare with similar fresh foods, the high quality cuts of meat which are most economical, and fish-meat comparisons. These and other such informative research will, of course, appeal most to men accompanying their wives or daughters who regularly do the shopping, and to the men who do their own and sometimes the family shopping. Women, however, seem to be instinctive in these matters.

Comparative shopping, without buying anything or very little, can be interesting if not especially challenging. And here you can range far beyond the usual daily or two-or-three-times-a-week shopping chores. You can get into lawn mowers, kitchen and laundry appliances, radios, TV sets, typewriters, sporting goods, cars, tools, building materials, cosmetics, and stationery. One way to do this is to make a list each week of ten or a dozen things the prices of which you want to compare and then sally forth to get the information.

Another aspect of shopping, somewhat akin to the foregoing, is to set yourself the task of finding where in town (or out of town) you can obtain almost anything you might want to buy and, where there are several shops or dealers which handle a product or service, the best place to buy it.

People vary in their attitudes toward shopping. Some enjoy visiting shops, and even enjoy shopping. Others want to avoid shopping like the plague, but find it difficult to avoid accompanying the family shopper.

In any event, if by choice or otherwise you find yourself involved with shopping, why not have *fun* doing it?

Time to Use

Being active, remaining active, uses time. But time is only to use. Many use it as an excuse for inactivity. "I haven't the time" and then proceed to waste the time they have. Inactivity uses just as much time as being active; and time spent in inactivity seems a lot longer.

There is the story of an older man-about-town who suffered poor health. After an examination, his doctor said to him, "I want you to stop smoking entirely; to quit drinking—not a drop; no gambling—it's too exciting; and no sexual activity!"

"Gosh, doctor, that's a very tough order. Will it prolong my life?"

"No, but it will *seem* a lot longer!"

At any age, at any time, in any situation, time is precious. An adage of some standing in duration and respect says that "time is money." Whether or not the good use of time can be translated directly into financial gain, it does have a distinct value—great value and increasing value.

From the age of fifty or there about, given today's expected life span, time becomes increasingly valuable as you grow older.

This, as with all other things of value, is due (along with demand) to scarcity. No matter how long you live, the number of years you will live is limited. Therefore, each year you live leaves one less year's time available. And the time available is thereby increasingly precious.

If you reflect on this and accept the thesis, you will never, never want to "*kill*" time, nor even *waste* it. This despite the fact that the many profligate do so. But none of us is really wealthy enough to afford this.

You will want to *use* your great (and free) asset, the precious time available to you, as *you* want to use it, and to good purpose.

You have a wealth of time to use—use it well!

> You say you have some time to kill?
> Please give that time to me;
> I have so very much to do
> I'll use it happily!

9   A Useful Purpose

The thoughts expressed in this chapter are related to and (to some extent) and extension of those in the preceding chapters "Keeping Mentally Alert," and "Remaining Active."

Mankind, like all other creatures, is naturally endowed with the ability and will to confront and resolve problems and obstacles. These qualities are necessary for survival. But mankind is distinguished from other creatures by his ability to look ahead beyond the confines and limitations of the present, the habitual, and the known, and by his imagination and intellectual curiosity, his ability to create and manage growth.

If an individual is to grow, to progress, he must use and sharpen his faculties and his abilities, he must have and accept challenges, he must confront and resolve problems. In short, he must have a useful purpose and attainable goals and objectives. This requires output, effort, thinking, *doing* something with the will to achieve.

You cannot live long after retirement if you then settle down to "just loafing," to "puttering" in the garden, to visiting the grandchildren, to traveling a little (without a purpose), to enjoying the sunshine on the beach, playing golf (in a cart—if you are up to that much exertion), going to the post office, helping with the shopping, and enjoying the increasingly varied fare appearing on the television tube. As a break, an interval, a diversion from exacting and purposeful tasks, such leisurely pastimes are good. But they are very bad as full-time occupations.

Let me repeat, for emphasis, what appears in the first chapter of this book, "The Retirement Syndrome." As head of an organization which did the honors at retirement parties, I presented the gift from colleagues, the company wallet, the good wishes from all. On such occasions I used to ask the new retirees what they planned to do now. The reply, with few exceptions, was, with only minor variations: "Well, I really haven't decided yet. I have no definite plans—I'll travel a little, visit the grandchildren, spend a little more time working in the garden and just loaf, I guess." I made a mental note "John will die of boredom in about two to three years." More often than not, he did. A little later, the company made a considerable effort to encourage and help its employees at all levels to prepare for an active and useful retirement.

Travelling, working in the garden, and other such usually casual and purposeless activities can be made meaningful. If, instead of sleeping less comfortably than at home and eating more pleasant but also more fattening and less nutritious meals, and otherwise passively absorbing what you see and a little of what you hear, you follow in your travels a plan of appraising the differences in the cultures of the lands you visit and comparing them with ours, or if you study some specific aspect of the foreign institutions, commerce, folkways, values, and people, then you have travelled with a purpose. You have acquired much that is good from your trip. And if you make notes, if you write about or prepare to speak on what you observed and learned, then your travel has, indeed, been worthwhile, has provided you with meaningful experience.

Likewise, if instead of "puttering" in the garden, you experiment with growing blue flowers from a variation of a seed that has always produced only red ones, and if you attempt to grow larger or smaller, more hardy, or in some other way a different variety of conventional vegetable, then again your efforts are directed toward meeting a challenge and achieving a meaningful and measurable goal.

The foregoing may be summarized in a broad concept of what is a useful purpose. In general, it would seem to require at least three basic elements:

(1) That the activity have *some element of compulsion and of responsibility and need.* It must not be a "now and then," "when I feel in the mood" kind of project, easily interrupted and abandoned and very low on the priority list. It should be something that requires regular concentrated attention and one that by its nature brooks no interference or suspension, except in a real emergency. Examples would be: daily, weekly, or even monthly writing a report, newspaper, or magazine article; teaching or attending a class at a community college; attending board of directors meetings; meeting as a member of a church vestry, and the like.

(2) That the project have a specific (or serious) purpose, and/or an *obtainable* goal. Using the examples mentioned in the preceding paragraph (1), all have a purpose or end that most would consider a useful contribution to the community or to self-improvement and, generally, to both. With respect to activities which have an attainable goal, these would be in the nature of studying to obtain a degree or certificate; planning and building an addition to one's home or a new structure on one's farm; completing a painting, story, poem, or book; planting a small field in corn or six vegetables in your garden, and so on.

(3) That the activity or project lend itself to *assessment of progress and achievement.* This means that it is sufficiently specific to know when the purpose or objective has been achieved, and that whenever it seems appropriate, the progress made can be easily determined.

10   *Your Friends*

When you reflect on it, you have really very few friends. All of us have a host of acquaintances. And they fall into fairly well-defined groups: social, business, civic, church, sport, school, and college. But friends, real friends, are only a handful—two, three, maybe five. These are people you are attached to by esteem, respect, and affection; those with whom you are intimate. Such a relationship develops only over a fairly long time. Actually, you have few *friends*.

And then where are your friends? One or two, perhaps, nearby and, therefore, currently, your best friend or friends. One or two are not close but within reasonably easy reach. The others, if any, are so far away as to warrant only the thought of a vacation visit and a Christmas card. This is the thing—old friends, good friends, move away (or you do) and die. So you seldom see most of your "good, old friends." You do see many *acquaintances* constantly.

Retired people appear to have two fixations with respect to friends. Both, I believe, are false.

(1) If you don't live near your friends, you will lose them.
(2) At this (retirement) age, you can't make new friends.

Since you have been separated from several, often most, and sometimes all of your real friends, due to their and/or your moves to new locations and new assignments, you are apt to see less and less of those whom you consider staunch friends. So, willy-nilly, you will lose old friends or you will have to make a special effort to keep in touch with them, regardless of whether or not you are retired.

As for making new friends from among new aquaintances, this is inevitable and natural. It will, of course, take time. And it will be pleasant and rewarding. It will require, also, some effort, some evaluation, some judgment.

With new friends (at your age) you need to distinguish carefully between an acquaintance, a congenial companion, and a friend. From a new friend, you will demand and expect more, you will be more critical, impatient and less tolerant (in this respect) than when you were younger. Then you were not so particular, so perceptive, so critical. Everyone was then your *friend*. If you are going to be selective (you should be and chances are good that you will be), you will, of course, make a number of false starts. The process, unquestionably, will involve trial and error. You will surely want to avoid being pushy or aggressive, and you will want to avoid those who are.

In the South, you must realize, the families which have lived there for generations take a dim view of Yankees; they are still, unfortunately, looked upon as invaders. A newcomer from north of the Mason-Dixon Line will be greeted cordially, treated with consideration and good manners, but not really liked or trusted. However, time is tempering this understandable view, and more and more Southerners are moving northward as more and more Northerners move southward. In the West and Midwest, the "newer" portions of our land, making friends is easier.

The age grouping of your friends (and acquaintances) comes into the picture again. Some feel strongly that they will be happy only with those in their own age range; others believe that they should associate largely with people substantially younger than they are (to the extent, at least, that this is practicable) to remain young at heart.

In the first instance, as the years go by you may, by natural attrition, run out of friends; in the second instance, you are apt to discover that the effort is neither appreciated by others nor rewarding to you. It follows naturally then that a sensible mixture of old and young friends provides the most satisfactory and stimulating reward.

Acquaintances you will almost necessarily have in good

numbers wherever you live. How many of these will develop into friends depends, at least largely, on *you*.

Briefly, the point about friends after retirement is:

(1) You will *not* lose your old friends.
(2) It is *not* difficult to make new friends.

11 Dollars and Sense

Your income on retirement is, and has to be an item of the greatest importance. How much it needs to be or should be will vary considerably with individuals. In most cases, although not in all, the amount you believe you need will be related to your income in the few years prior to your retirement. Your retirement income obviously has to be sufficient to permit you to live in the manner in which you plan or planned to live and influenced largely by how you have been living just prior to retirement.

If the amount you believe you need to live comfortably in retirement exceeds what you will receive in retirement salary, social security, return on investments and savings, and other sources, you have a problem. The solution is evident. You will have to earn or somehow produce additional income or you will have to reduce expenses. The first is difficult, the second option is difficult and also painful. Obviously, it doesn't matter what your income is or what you spend as long as the two are in balance.

To put this matter in proper focus, permit me to relate a personal experience bearing on the subject. A friend in an upper-middle-management position with a large corporation announced that he would retire early at the minimum age at which he could receive a retirement salary. This was five years before the mandatory retirement age. He planned to move to the land he had acquired in central Virginia, where he would build a house and farm.

"That doesn't seem very intelligent," remarked one of the

small group he addressed. "With this escalating inflation your salary will be increased materially in the next five years even if you don't get a merit increase or two. And, of course, you will lose five years credit in the computation of your retirement salary. That's about twelve percent. You seem deliberately to be throwing away a substantial portion of your retirement income."

"Yes," he replied, "if you look at it that way, you are quite right. But I don't.

"What income I lose by retiring early is academic. These next five years, at my age, are very valued ones. The chief consideration is, will I have enough money to live the way I want to in Virginia? Actually, income-wise, that is my *only* concern. And, I might add, I can live on my Virginia farm in a more leisurely and generally satisfactory, comfortable and enjoyable manner than I experience in New York at about half of what it costs me to live here.

"And if I do work here for another five years—sure, I earn a lot of money, but the 'take-home' portion isn't much; the expenses eat it all up. And in addition, I'm a candidate for ulcers and whatever it is you get from breathing foul air and being unduly crowded. Money is only to be used, to be spent; and I will get a great deal more for much less money farming than I will working in New York.

"So long boys, I'm through here—much as I've enjoyed it— and I'm about to start living the way I want to!"

The sources of your retired income will include one, several, or all of these: (1) retired salary, (2) social security, (3) income from a variety of investments, (4) royalties, (5) capital gains from sales of property or other assets, (6) rent, (7) annuities, (8) paid-up or cancelled life insurance, and (9) earnings from new endeavors or new employment.

The amount of income you need to live in the manner you want to is controlling. You know what you will receive from the above sources without effort on your part. If you need to earn more than that to live as you want to, you may (1) seek employment for a salary or fee, (2) establish a small (or large) business enterprise (including farming, breeding horses or cattle, dairying, and similar projects), and (3) invest for profit or income.

Let us review each of the sources of income separately.

Retired Salary

This is usually fixed and known. As a rule, it varies with your salary during your last several active years of employment and whether or not you contributed to your firm's retirement income plan. Usually your only option is when to retire within the latitude provided by the company's plan. That is, you need to balance the loss of retirement salary by retiring "early" against the need for income from this source and the value to you of an "early" retirement. Some employers make periodic adjustments in the amount of their pension payments to cover increases in the cost of living caused by inflation. More do not.

Social Security Payments from the Federal Government

What you will receive from this source is also known. From time to time, however, the amount of these payments is increased slightly with increases in the cost of living. It has the considerable advantage of being tax free.

You have an "early" option also with social security payments. Under existing regulations, if you are not employed, you may apply at age sixty-two rather than sixty-five when you will receive the maximum for which you qualify, and receive about 75 percent of the amount you would receive at age sixty-five. The smaller amount received should be balanced against the three additional years income from this source and how you will use it.

Problems with respect to social security payments arise (at any rate until you reach seventy-two years of age) if you are employed by others or are self-employed. The regulations permit you to earn a specified amount while receiving social security payments. Each additional $100 a month incurs a loss of one dollar of social security payment for each two dollars earned over this specified amount. Your earnings in excess of the specified amount may well result in your receiving no social security payments. The amount you are permitted to earn without affecting or losing your social security payments has been increased several times and, if rapid inflation continues, it will probably be increased again. Obviously, then, you need to consider carefully any offers of employment or engagement in a business of your own, with reference to the corresponding loss of social security payments. You might find that you are about to work with no increase in income. And be sure to consider the value of the tax free aspects of your social security income!

Income from Investments

With respect to *income* from your investments, decisions would seem to be required in only two areas: (1) can you otherwise invest the capital producing the income you now receive with equal safety, to produce a greater income, and (2) can you invest or reinvest these funds with a reasonable certainty of greater profit through capital gains?

Therefore, thinking about, planning, and managing your investments would, in general, be little different from what these were before retirement. In two areas, however, somewhat new (or, at least, intensified) problems arise.

After retirement, the need is greater to determine and decide how much of your invested capital should be used for current expenditures—to meet the expense of establishing and improving a new home, for travel, perhaps even to supplement regular monthly income. Several "systematic withdrawal" investment trusts (mutual funds) are oriented to such a procedure. After all, you can't take it with you. Chances are that your children are earning (or at any rate receiving) a substantially greater income than you did at the same age, even making allowance for the decreased purchasing power of the dollar.

Then, too, you will probably want to reexamine and restudy your investments to orient them to the greatest extent toward income with reasonable safety. In addition, your policy with respect to reinvestment (switching) to produce income from capital gains will need to be restudied. Since the support and flexibility of your investment for profit provided by a monthly salary or the earning from a business enterprise are reduced on retirement, you need more carefully to balance return, the prospects of profit from a sale and security. You can (and, of course, will) still take calculated risks, but not, wisely, to the extent you did prior to retirement.

It is well to keep in mind that with a reduced income, your tax bracket and your income tax will be less and, therefore, your capital gains will cost less. In this connection, be sure to take advantage of the situation by taking capital gains a year *after* your retirement.

It goes without saying that you will be well served to seek competent advice and guidance by presenting your situation and discussing your financial objectives with an established investment firm and/or your bank.

Triple A corporate and government bonds can be bought from time to time at prices to yield attractive returns (8 to 9 percent) with great security. The trouble with bonds (debt capital) is that their fixed income in periods of continued or rapid inflation is a considerable limitation and their appreciation in times of decreasing interest rates is seldom substantial, as is their loss of value in a period of rising interest rates. In addition, sound bonds bearing high interest coupons are generally ''called'' (redeemed at a stated price in excess of the face value) when interest rates remain substantially lower than the coupon.

Short term (six months) notes issued by the Federal government or one of its agencies and yielding a relatively high return are usually available. In an uncertain securities market, investment in these securities may prove advantageous—until the market stabilizes.

Almost everyone has a dream—to write a best selling novel, and/or to make a killing in the stock market, as a sure way to wealth.

If you are of a mind to "take a flyer" in the "put and call" market or in the commodity exchange, don't do it! A few full-time experienced professionals do make a comfortable living, winning some, losing some, in these high-risk ventures. But most—about 85 percent, a securities broker friend of mine told me—lose substantially.

If you want to "play" the stock market and can afford a moderate loss of both income and capital appreciation from this source, try this simple, satisfactory, and in the long run profitable procedure. It is not glamorous, it will not make you a millionaire, but you can well average 20 percent or better on your investments in the securities market.

Select ten (or six, or twelve) of the basic industrial corporations from among the first fifty (or 100 if you prefer) of "Fortune" magazine's list of the leading 500 U.S. corporations. Make your selections in varying fields—utilities, oils, motors, chemicals, steel, aluminum, business machines, pharmaceuticals, and others. It is interesting, for an example, that the common stock of American Telephone and Telegraph Company and Exxon frequently move in opposite directions, since many consider Exxon a hedge against inflation, and A.T. and T. a hedge against deflation.

Having selected first-rate successful companies which have been in business a long time and are not soon apt to go out of business, you now determine at what price each will be an advantageous investment. A simple procedure for making this determination is:

(1) Average the corporation's annual earnings per share over the last three years, weighting this a little toward the last and current years' earnings. Multiply this by seven. (A price-earnings ratio of seven. PE's are published for all traded stocks listed by the New York Stock Exchange in The Wall Street Journal.) Note this price, to the lower whole number.

(2) Average the corporation's annual dividends over the last three years, again weighting in favor of the current payout. Now compute the price at which the stock would produce a 7 percent return (or 7½ percent). It works this way. Assume that the ABC Corporation is, and has for the last three years, been paying an annual dividend of $2.10. Then, to yield a 7 percent return, its stock would have to be bought at $30 a share; to yield 7½ percent, it would have to be acquired at $28 per share.

(3) Average the price obtained under procedures (1) and (2) to the lower whole number.

At the thus determined price, if the corporation does not reduce its dividends (most large corporations have sufficiently adequate reserves not to do so), you can be unconcerned with the stocks' day-to-day and month-to-month fluctuations.

At the same time you purchase a quantity of one of the six, ten, or twelve selected stocks at your specified price, instruct your broker to sell the shares when the price reaches a figure ten points higher than what you paid for the stock. With the proceeds place an order for your determined "good buy" price on another of your six to twelve selections which at the time is nearest your price.

This way you will have fun and make a little money with a minimum of worry or risk.

Apropos of this, the astute and successful financier J. P. Morgan was asked the secret of success for investing in the stock market. He replied succinctly, "It is quite simple. I'll tell you, with assurance that you will not follow my advice. The two basic principles are: (1) don't attempt to buy at the bottom or to sell at the top; (2) you can only make money taking a profit!" How many people are miserable because of, "If I had just waited another week, I could have bought it for three points less"; "If I had only held it for another week, I could have sold it for three dollars more a share!"? You can't rely on hindsight and you should not be greedy!

A final word on the matter of invested funds. Personal temperament, emotional characteristics, psychology—call it what you will—plays an important role at all times. After retirement, because of more time to think about one's investments and a greater dependence on them, the psychology of investment is an even more important consideration. In this respect, then, you need to balance investment in equity securities (common stocks) with their often substantial profit potential, with the concern, worry and anxiety their ownership might generate.

If you study the Wall Street Journal daily, subscribe to financial magazines and newsletters, and are frequently in touch with your broker, you may wish to consider the stress, strain and increased blood pressure such preoccupation costs you. Perhaps fixed income investments would also buy considerable peace of mind; a desirable profit indeed.

Royalties

If you receive royalties from writing or the ownership of land rich in natural resources, you will, of course, continue to receive them. In some instances they will increase, in others they will diminish. No comment appears warranted.

An incident on the light side, pertaining to the subject, might prove interesting.

A well-educated man who had sold a few stories to a magazine and published one book, became friendly with an especially attractive young woman. She was long on all the feminine qualities but quite obviously a little lacking in conventional schooling. At one point in a conversation she remarked casually and in passing on her royalties. "Royalties," thought the man to himself, "why this delight can't even write a good letter." Then he asked her, "What is the name of your book?"

"Book?", she repeated with a gracious smile and her eyes wide with consternation. "Whatever made you think I wrote a book, honey?"

"Well, I just wondered about your royalties."

"Oh, them? They're from oil they found on our little ranch in Texas!"

Capital Gains from the Sale of Property or Other Assets

The basic problem is whether to sell, hold, or change. Considerations related to these are: (1) opportunities for income production without selling; (2) a reasonable and realistic price; (3) when and in what market to sell; and (4) tax advantages.

Income from New Employment or a Personal Business Venture (Supplementing Your Retirement Income)

Such income may be a necessity, because it and other combined income is not sufficient to cover the expenditures needed to live as you wish to. On the other hand, primarily to keep busy and to continue an occupation or hobby you enjoy, you may engage in a post-retirement activity which produces substantial income, even though you may well be able to get along without it.

Most people, when they retire, have a sufficient income to live in the manner in which they had planned. However, rapid inflation and (ironically) the sharply increased taxes, which are supposed to slow the inflation, have combined to reduce these incomes to such an extent that many retired people are faced with the choice of seeking additional income or materially reducing their standard of living.

The need to supplement their retirement incomes is especially acute among those who continue to live in the same location and attempt to live in the same manner as they did prior to retirement, and people in the armed services of our country who retire after twenty or even thirty years of service with children still in or about to go to college.

Those fortunate enough not to *have* to supplement their retirement income will find, nonetheless, that employment for a salary or fee, or engaging in a business venture for profit, provides special satisfaction and recognition.

So, whether your motivation is a need to earn some money or only to accept the challenge of doing something which others consider sufficiently productive to warrant a fee or salary, it may be well to review the employment situation for retirees.

The opportunities available to competent retired persons are many, attractive, and adequately compensatory. The situation develops a happy two-way bargain. Because of his assured retirement income, a retired person can afford to accept a responsible job at considerably less compensation than an equally competent man who must rely on the job as his only or primary source of income. On the other hand, his employer acquires competence at a cost materially less than what he would have to pay a nonretired person.

Universities and schools especially welcome competent retired people in both teaching and administrative jobs in order to make the most of their limited funds. For the same reason hospitals, and municipal and county governments and agencies, are eager to employ you. Small- and medium-sized businesses offer a number of opportunities, particularly in the part-time and specialty fields.

The larger business and industrial concerns hesitate to take on older people (forty and up) because of their pension plans, union agreements, and promotion-from-within policies in supervisory and middle management positions at any rate. On the other hand, the industrial and business giants will frequently take on men and women who have retired early from top level posts in other enterprises to fill regular positions or as consultants. General officers of the Army, Marine Corps, and Air Force and Flag officers of the Navy fare especially well in this respect, and so also do junior officers and warrant officers.

Retired technical, industrial, and business specialists (engineers, forecasters, analysts, accountants, and computer programmers) are much sought after by firms in foreign lands and by several of our own government agencies operating primarily abroad. These jobs are, naturally, of a limited duration, but the remuneration is extremely attractive and a certain adventure attaches to them.

The Peace Corps provides a number of opportunities for retired people. The adventure and the satisfaction of helping the underprivileged in developing countries is very attractive, but the monetary compensation (largely expenses) is on the low side. But remember that you don't have to spend any of your retirement income!

The United States armed services and other government agencies publish periodicals and a number of pamphlets designed to assist their people in finding suitable jobs in retirement. From time to time they also hold conferences on adjustment to retirement and job opportunities.

A number of private employment agencies cater to the placement of retired people and several ''executive search'' organizations will help find a place for an especially able retiree.

The greatest field for retired people is, of course, a large variety of businesses with which they can become associated on a commission-remuneration basis. Typical of these are insurance, real estate, placement, and selling everything from soft goods to automobiles and appliances. To engage in some of these activities requires a license, and you must pass an examination to obtain it. This should not be an obstacle.

Public relations, personal counseling, and financial analysis offer attractive opportunities to those experienced and successful in these fields.

Let us look at employment for a retired person who *needs* to supplement his income from *his* point of view.

First, if you are sixty-two or older you need to reckon with your social security payments. These are tax exempt and therefore exceed their face value. If you earn over a certain amount (always increasing) you lose some of your social security payment, and if you earn over the maximum amount you lose it all.

And, if you accept a job offer, you need to figure the cost of transportation, lunches, club and association memberships (even if the dues and direct business expense are absorbed by your employer), an increased clothing budget, and such.

To return to social security, assume that your social security payment (retiring at 65) is, for example, $460 per month or about $5,500 per year. If you are offered an annual salary of $8,000, you are really only supplementing your income by about $6,000 (because you lose a dollar of social security for each $2 you earn over $4,000). And bear in mind that the $8,000 is taxed while the social security payment is not. There are, of course, gimmicks, like doing all of the work for which you receive remuneration in one or more months, but this is tricky. And there may be some tax penalties for employment at a low level, such as losing retired pay credit which is applied directly to the gross tax. The point here is to check your situation with a lawyer, an accountant, or the social security advisers paid by the Federal government to help you. They do an intelligent and sympathetic job in your interest.

As a retired person, an important consideration is whether you wish to (and should) work *full time* or *part time.* Unhappily, but unavoidably, necessity usually answers the question. If you can afford to work part time (generally this means *half time*), it is obviously a better arrangement in that it is a welcome break from the preretirement necessity and because it permits you a wider range of interests. Part-time employment is more consistent with the character of the retired person as an independent businessman, a free lance, an uncommitted business person, than is a full-time job. It seems strange (but maybe it isn't) that you are apt to receive almost as much remuneration for part-time assignments as for a full-time one!

If you can arrange and can afford part-time employment, be sure, where this is reasonable and satisfactory, to specify that the part time is at *your* discretion. Only thus do you reap the greatest benefit from the arrangement. You will, of course, a) assure your employer that the job required will be done to his great satisfaction and than, b) naturally, you will put in such specific hours as the job or an emergency requires, but that c) by and large, you may be in the office in the morning one day and the afternoon the next, or d) all day Monday and not at all on Tuesday, or e) all of this week, but not next, and so on provided, of course, that the nature of the job permits this. On the other hand, if a special situation requires you to be in all day every day, that you will do this too (and without charge!). Place emphasis on doing a good job—not on the time spent in doing it.

Perhaps the most important factor in a new job after retirement is your personal competence from the standpoint of both your employer and you. Certainly there is nothing more damaging to one's mental and physical health and general well being than doubt, uncertainty, lack of confidence, and associated disturbances. And certainly no one should accept a job for which he or she does not feel fully qualified and confident.

A word on resumés. Normally, but not always (depending on your reputation), one is required. Regardless of the requirement, it seems desirable to submit one. Make it brief and significant, use as few words as practicable, and try hard to keep it on one page. (Recall Voltaire's (I believe) pithy comment, ''Please excuse this long letter, I didn't have time to write a short one.'') Include education, business experience, and accomplishments, military record, decorations, and awards, civic activities and honors, and publications, if any.

Most important, though, is to start with a carefully thought through succinct, and informative ''*Area of Competence.*'' This should come first, right after the vital statistics.

In short, if you need to supplement your income, you should have no trouble finding a job. Determining whether or not it is a job that suits you, challenges and absorbs your interest and attention, and whether it really produces sufficient additional income requires real study. The answer, as always, is up to you!

Saving and Spending

Ask the average person what he or she thinks children should be taught about money, whether how to *save* it or *spend* it, and the reply will be ''save it.'' You would probably receive the same reply if you asked the question of young adults.

When we speak about saving money, most of us think about holding out a portion of one's income and putting it in a savings bank, investing in securities, joining a Christmas Club, buying an annuity, and cash benefits in connection with life insurance, paying off a mortgage, and other debts. This is saving for a ''rainy day,'' for the future. Surely this is sound advice and sound practice.

But the catch is, where do you get the money to save? Perhaps we are putting the cart before the horse.

The best way to have money to save is to spend wisely and well. By thinking, planning, being alert to opportunities, making a little extra effort, you can reduce your expenditures 10 to 30 percent of what you might spend otherwise. This saving in spending can then be used for "rainy day" saving.

So, how do you save by spending wisely? There are four basic elements in spending which, for this purpose, we will restrict to buying. They are: (1) *what* you buy; (2) *how much* you buy; (3) *when* you buy it; and, (4) the *price*. The first three are controllable—by you. Sometimes, by bargaining and dealing, so is the price.

There are, of course, certain fixed expenses over which you have very little or no control; rent, or payments on the mortgage, insurance, utilities, and taxes, for examples. With thought, research, shopping, and comparing, some of these might have cost you less than you are paying, but now you are committed to them. Most of the other monthly expenditures can be controlled. This group is large and variable. It includes at least these: food, beverages, cigarettes, clothes, cleaning, cosmetic services, fuel for home and automobiles, the doctor, dentist and medical supplies, education, travel and entertainment, clubs and associations, magazine and newspaper subscriptions.

The trick is to achieve economy without materially reducing your standard of living.

What you buy and spend, other than for fixed and committed items, is largely a matter of listing priorities, estimating the cost of each item, and balancing the two against funds available for them. And, in this connection, *quality* should receive high consideration. In the long run, the quality product (frequently not the most expensive) outlasts, and is more satisfying and less expensive, than a cheaper one of inferior quality. Many products sold in "chain" stores, under their own name, are identical with substantially more expensive well-advertised brand names. Mouthwash, toothpaste, soap, vitamins, and tools are a few of them.

How large a quantity to get of what you buy (how much to buy) depends on the price advantage of a larger quantity, on room and facilities to store it, and the chances of spoilage and deterioration. Larger containers of many products are, naturally, less expensive than small ones and many products are advertised at a lower price if you buy two or four or half a dozen. But in the latter case, be sure that you will and can profitably, use the extras. On the farm, many expendables are substantially less expensive by the ton or truckload than in 100 pound units—if you have the facilities to store and handle them.

When to buy requires watching advertisements in the press and on radio and television, and on scheduling your shopping trips to minimize their frequency and thus save human and fuel energy. Many items, especially in the food and drugstore categories, are on "special" sometime or other. Sometimes a shop owner or manager will let you know in advance, if you ask. Other obvious opportunities for saving through timing are to purchase summer items in the fall and winter items in the spring and summer, and to take advantage of "after Christmas" and other such sales, and so-called "preinventory" sales—provided, of course, they are genuine. Such sales are particularly advantageous in the clothing (if you are not overly fashion conscious), sporting goods, and furniture areas.

The *price*, we said, is sometimes, but not often, negotiable. The best price is obtained when the item you want is on sale, a "special" and in an "off" season. But be wary of sales and "specials." Be sure that the content and *quality* are what you want. The best bargains are in established brand items of which you know the usual price so that you can determine how much of a bargain you are getting.

Why did I omit *where* to buy? Because this depends upon where you live and the shops in your area. You can, of course, visit *all* in your area to find the lowest price for each item on your shopping list, but the time, energy and gasoline consumed make this procedure one of very dubious advantage.

There are, of course, some areas in which savings cannot or should not be made. These would include a mortgage, other debts, insurance, medical expenses, rent, and home maintenance (I do not suggest so drastic a saving as moving to a less attractive home), and other expenses of this nature. Even in these areas, however, some savings are possible through "shopping" for the best or better rates, consolidation, lengthening or shortening commitments, and such. But there are a number of areas in which a close review and study will indicate several opportunities for saving which, surprisingly, are relatively painless and can, like regular physical exercise, be a fun challenge. These areas include largely: food, beverages, entertaining, clothes, your car, club and association dues, magazine and newspaper subscriptions. There are, of course, others. It seems unwise to economize in an area that would actually reduce your standard of living, when you can be careful to spend wisely and make minor modifications in your spending in the interest of economy.

The following are some further opportunities for savings in specific areas.

Food

There are three areas in which you can reduce your food costs and probably gain advantages in weight control and nutritional value.

You can buy the least expensive in a line of related foods. For example, if you enjoy pork for breakfast, you might compare the price (for a comparable quantity) of bacon, ham, and sausage to your advantage, and also inquire into the difference in price for the same quality among the different brands and independent packers. Frequently there are local sources of good quality and at a reasonable price. You might also find it advantageous cost wise to compare both the merits and price of various cuts of meat and the variation in price of fresh vegetables related to the day of purchase. A keen eye and ear for advertised bargains (and a good acquaintance with the manager) might give you advance notice of sales, "specials" and other economies. Probably all of this can be summarized by "smart shopping."

Study and research into the relative nutritional characteristics and values of various foods could reduce your budget for meals and reduce your doctor bills as well. There are a number of excellent books on the subject.

Finally, it makes an interesting game to put together a meal that is at the same time appetizing and economical. Then plan to enjoy one of your economy meals once a week, or twice. You can, of course extend the game, by creating economy breakfasts, lunches, and dinners and having an economy day or an economy breakfast Monday, an economy dinner Wednesday, and an economy lunch on Friday. And if fish, chicken, or a cut or kind of meat is relatively inexpensive in your area or on certain days, with only a little determination, you *could* learn to like these not always distinguished and over familiar foods!

Beverages

Economy here involves quantity, quality, type, packaging, and price. It requires study, comparative shopping, and comparative tasting. Beverages include a large number of drinkables in several classifications: tea, coffee, milk, soft drinks, and "mixes," fruit and vegetable juices, wines, beer, and a variety of "hard" liquors.

In the more expensive beverages, be sure that the well-advertised and respected label (probably based on a carefully nurtured snob appeal) is worth what you are paying for it. A wholesale dealer in Scotch whiskies, when I asked him which was the best buy, smiled wryly and replied, "Well, with a few exceptions, the Scotch whiskey imported here comes from four large distillers. In bulk it costs somewhere in the order of eighty cents a gallon. Now you have to add import duty, shipping, handling, warehousing, transportation, bottling and packaging, wholesaler commissions, and (most expensive) advertising! Now you figure out what the difference in quality is!"

If you can store them conveniently, larger containers provide obvious savings. Your liquid requirements, from milk to whiskey, will cost less if purchased in gallon, half-gallon, or quart containers than in smaller containers.

But beware, from the viewpoint of economy, of discounts for the purchase of case lots. You are very apt to lose the profit quickly through using much more because it is handy and "cheap." If you want to preserve the savings of case-lot purchases, be sure that you strictly ration the number of cans or bottles you will use daily or weekly and keep the rest of the case somewhere hard to get at.

"House brands" frequently compare favorably in quality and taste with nationally advertised brands and are materially less expensive.

Entertaining

How things are served, the table setting, atmosphere, and the company in which they are served is as important (probably much more important) than what is served and how it tastes. There may certainly be opportunities for economy in each of these basic aspects of entertaining, but concentrating efforts to save in the what is served department, however, would seem to have a better chance of saving with success.

The relative cost of one large party as against several smaller ones may be revealing. It is worth looking into. And it might be productive to consider the relative expense of entertaining at breakfast, lunch, and dinner. Breakfast and luncheon parties (except that usually they have to be confined to weekends and holidays) can be even gayer than dinner parties, and they are bound to be a lot less expensive.

Entertaining "out" (at a club or public restaurant) saves a lot of trouble and worry, of course, but you pay heavily for the luxury. So, steel yourself to entertaining at home, do it well, and learn to enjoy it. When you do entertain away from home (and sometimes you must) select the meal and agree on a fixed price, including gratuities. Your guests are apt to enjoy this more than having to choose their meal from a menu. And it seems more thoughtful and courteous to your guests to arrange their meal for them.

Clothes

This area provides comparatively little room for saving as such since the only practical economy is to postpone further purchases. For a woman this poses some difficult problems, but a style-conscious person can, with imagination, effort and determination, almost make a silk purse out of a sow's ear. For a man, a good tailor can put a seemingly outdated but still-serviceable suit right back in style.

The only other clothes economy, at any rate for a man, is to rotate neckties, have them cleaned frequently, and press them at home. Doing this assures a long life for your favorites, which are difficult and expensive to duplicate. And rotating the wearing of suits so that they may "hang out their wrinkles" will save something on pressing bills.

To "shop around" for the least expensive item of clothing almost always results in finding that the comparatively cheapest one is lacking in quality and style. You can, however, save on the purchase of new clothes by waiting for sales in your favorite shop. Also, by buying needed winter items in the spring, and summer items in the fall, you can achieve worthwhile savings.

Your Car

The controllable expense of a motor car is largely (almost entirely) in repairs and replacement parts and in miles per gallon of fuel.

The cost of repairs, unfortunately and improperly, varies unbelievably, depending on who does the job. Broadly, you have a choice between a local small garage mechanic who may or may not be competent, but who is reasonably sure to make a fair and modest charge for his work, and a dealer's service department, where the hired help may or may not be competent but usually are and where you are sure to be charged considerably more than by the independent garage mechanic. Again, much questioning of patrons, trial and error, and keen perception is required to find the best place to have your car serviced. There are too, as you would expect, although few, some real gyps. *Caveat emptor!*

Your research in this field will pay big dividends.

Club and Association Dues

There may be some profit in reviewing these each year. It is hard to give up the associations implicit in your memberships and you tend to rationalize them as costing really very little. And then you never know when it might just be very important to use your club. You might, on the other hand, figure what it costs you per meal, per drink, per round of golf, or per evening!

At retirement age, even if it is early and you are comparatively young, you are not trying to make points, establish standing in the community, or build stature; you have all of that you will get. So, balance your dues with the number of times you have availed yourself of your club's facilities and privileges. No doubt there are some social club and association memberships you may well drop. As an alternative you can, at least, transfer to an out-of-town or limited membership, to the extent that this option is available.

It is, of course, convenient and pleasant to use your club—to be able to ask friends, out-of-town visitors, and business acquaintances to meet you there for lunch or for a drink. But, even though you won't realize it until the end of the month, it *is* costly. It might pay to review your club bills and practice a reasonable restraint.

Bills

It seems odd to suggest that you can save money paying bills. But it is true that you can. And I don't mean discounts for prompt payment and avoiding penalties for late payment, although these should be considered.

You can "save" by earning interest from a savings bank or a savings and loan association through depositing money used later to pay bills. Here is an example:

Your electricity bill will fluctuate considerably. Unless you have an expensive air conditioning installation in your home your electric bills (except for homes in the deep South) will usually be considerably less in the summer months than in the winter months. Determine for the latest twelve-month period the amount of your average monthly bill. Starting with the first month for which the bill is *less* than the average, pay the electric company's bill and deposit the difference between your payment and the average bill in a savings account to draw interest. Continue this (through the summer and early fall) until the bill reaches close to your average. When the bill substantially exceeds the average, write a check for the average amount and draw the remainder from your savings account. The interest earned on your deposits in the subaverage months will reduce the amount of your electric bills for the twelve-month period. Many electric companies are glad to issue "level" bills throughout the year, based on your estimated average usage, but they pay no interest.

You may apply the same procedure to the payment of your insurance premiums and taxes. These are usually payable quarterly or annually. Budget the average monthly amounts of these payments and deposit these amounts in your savings account until the payment is due. And you may as well leave that amount in the bank until a few days before a penalty for late payment is incurred. For example, most insurance premium payments have a thirty-day "grace" period. You will earn additional interest if you pay the premium five days before the end of the grace period. In doing this you must be careful to mail (or make) your payment promptly on the day selected.

An amusing application of the saving through a savings account deposit principle was practiced by a friend of mine confronted with a penalty for not paying a real estate tax bill before the deadline. Before leaving on an out-of-town trip, he instructed his (commercial) bank to pay the upcoming tax bill. He found on his return that through some misunderstanding, the bank had failed to comply with his request. He obtained a check for the required amount and presented it to the appropriate clerk at city hall. This occurred only one day beyond the deadline. He explained the situation, but the clerk and his supervisor politely insisted that he must, in addition, pay a 5 percent penalty.

"All right," said my friend, "how long have I to pay the tax with the penalty?"

"Until April 30th," replied the clerk. (It was then December 6th.)

"O.K.," said my friend. "I'll pay you on the 29th of April. I'm going to put this check in my savings account. The interest I earn during those almost five months will pay a good portion of your penalty."

Pills, Powders, Pastes and Lotions

All of us constantly need bathroom supplies and cosmetics, and most of us now take one or another vitamin and mineral supplements. All of these can be, and usually are, purchased at the "chain" drugstores and supermarkets.

Substantial savings may be realized in these emporiums in three ways.

(1) Buying needed items when they are on sale. Reduction in the usual price is considerable.
(2) Buying what you need in the largest convenient container.
(3) Buying the store's own brand. Such items as toothpaste, mouthwashes, soap, skin "conditioners," and vitamins and minerals are substantially less expensive than nationally advertised brands. In one instance, I compared the ingredients of a well-known and nationally advertised high potency multivitamin and mineral capsule with similar products sold by a drugstore chain and a regional supermarket. The ingredients listed were identical to the exact milligram. The capsules even looked alike. The only difference was in the name and packaging—and the price.

Fuel Consumption

With the rapid and continuing rise in the cost of fuel, you have a keen challenge to reduce the cost of heating your home, the cost of operating your several time- and muscle-saving appliances, and of reducing the amount of fuel burned by your automobile.

Advice on effective means of accomplishing reductions in the use of energy by homeowners is readily available in pamphlets published by a variety of local and federal government agencies and by the fuel companies themselves.

Accomplishing savings in these areas is not easy. But the effort provides interesting challenges and is especially rewarding financially.

Magazine and Newspaper Subscriptions

Most of us are heavily oversubscribed. Magazines and news-papers pile up unopened and unwrapped to be thrown away unscanned from a few weeks to a year or two later. Some are glanced through and never read. At retirement age, no useful (nor artistic) purpose is served in purchasing class, "highbrow," and prestigeous periodicals merely to display them.

An obvious and simple test to determine which subscriptions to cancel is to reflect on which you have devoted more than thirty minutes over the last four issues.

Keep in mind, too, that any magazines you have at home are normally available at your public library, at a nearby high school or college, at your dentist's and doctor's offices, at the hairdresser and barber, and at your club. And remember that important news and features are syndicated and are apt to appear in your local newspaper so that you need not subscribe to a big city newspaper to be *au courant*. Then there are the radio and TV to keep you well posted and amused.

Senior Citizen Discounts

In many localities, the town, city, or county (or a special group organized for the purpose) has arranged with stores, service businesses, and cinema theaters to provide discounts, usually in the order of 10 percent, to "senior citizens" presenting an identification card issued by the sponsoring political or private organization.

A "senior citizen" is usually defined as a person sixty years of age and older—employed or not. Some may rebel against being classified as a "senior citizen" and those and others may object to being what they consider subjects of "charity." Understandable. But, if viewed as an earned privilege of those largely dependent on a fixed income in these days of little-controlled inflation, one can easily swallow his or her pride. And remember that the shop or service you patronize finds the 10 percent discount inexpensive advertising.

The freely offered opportunity to save a little seems worth accepting.

Strictly You

There are a number of reputable consumer unions and associations which make available to their members research on the relative quality, durability, and cost of consumer goods and appliances. An investment in, and study of these should be enlightening and fruitful.

The best guide as to where to concentrate your money-saving efforts is, of course, a monthly and cumulative comparison of actual expenditures against what has been budgeted for each item.

There is, certainly, some gold, maybe a lot of it, "in them there bills." Why not go after it? It is sure to be a rewarding and profitable adventure. Pursuing it with a good attitude should also make the adventure an enjoyable one.

A final comment on the matter of dollars and good sense: Be sure that you operate on a budget; Remember that a budget is *not* a statement of what you want to, or think you should spend, but rather *how* to spend the money you have available; And, unlike our Federal government's, it needs to be strictly in balance!

12   *Possessions*

We all have a little of the squirrel in us. We are apt to save all sorts of currently useless things—paper bags, plastic containers, string, tacks, bottles, cans, boxes, bags, towels, broken tools, surplus furniture, and whatnot—with the thought that one day they may come in handy for something.

The saving of unused, unusable, and useless things is most marked in the area of clothes, books, papers, momentos, and in jewelry, silver, linen, and glassware.

If a suit or a dress no longer fits, is out of style, or is in a disliked color or a little worn or shabby, you are apt to clutter the closet with it instead of discarding it ''just in case'' or with the thought that you will only wear it around the house or for work clothes to save the clothing you enjoy wearing. Actually, the undesirable suit or dress hangs undisturbed in the closet for years. Certainly it is unrewarding and unsatisfactory to wear worn, ill-fitting, and unliked clothing when you have similar clothing you do like. If you feel that thereby, however, you are ''saving'' your good clothing, ask yourself—saving it for what and when? And remember that you can give your unwanted clothes to the Salvation Army, other charitable institutions, and to your church and obtain a tax credit.

Careful and honest examination will disclose many duplicates and unused items among your jewelry, china, glassware, flat silver or plate, towels, bed linen, and other such possessions. Some of your children, grandchildren, friends, and charitable institutions no doubt will be happy to have the surplus, duplicate, and unused among these items. And, if no one wants them (and you don't use them) then screw up your courage and sell them to a dealer or junk man.

Books of dubious literary value and of no use for reference —some read, some partially read, some unread—are apt to clutter tables, desks, and already crowded bookcases. It takes courage to discard these. It might be helpful to consider the credit you will receive as a civic-minded benefactor if you give these no longer used books to a local library or hospital or school.

Unread magazines are always a great clutter, especially as most of us subscribe to more than we can possibly read. The trick here is, of course, to throw the previous issue away as soon as the new issue arrives. But how few do this. Nearly all of us stack up the unread back numbers to read on a rainy day. As a compromise between keeping unread periodicals and discarding them, you might tear out and save the articles you believe will prove interesting and informative. This will reduce the bulk of stacked paper for future (if ever!) reading.

With respect to momentos and clippings, you need first to decide whether or not they are worth keeping. If they really are (and you should put each promptly to a severe test), fasten them to appropriate pages of loose leaf books designed for this purpose. If you do not, they are likely to be piled here and there to be mutilated and lost.

The foregoing, I recognize, applies to adults of all ages, both occupied and retired. But for retired people the need for and oportunity to reduce possessions, to get rid of surplus, duplicate, and unused things is greater, much greater, than for the regularly employed. A good guide to success is to discard anything you have not used, worn, or read, no matter how much *possible* use you can see for it at *sometime*. For how long? Say two years—maybe one?

Even though it is difficult, you can make getting rid of clutter a very worthwhile and challenging project. The reward will be considerably more living room, greater "maneuver" space, a reduced number of material things to keep track of and maintain, knowing what you have in the way of tangible things and where they are, greater use of the good things you have, and the great feeling of freedom that always results from carrying only a little luggage and owning only a few valued things.

A contingent reward is that you may turn up something valuable you did not know you had, or something you thought had been lost.

13 *Your Home*

Few people in our highly mobile society have strong, if any, roots, any place they call "home" for any length of time or to which one day they wish to return. Few want roots. Job requirements cause most of us to move frequently during our working careers. And the moves are generally long distances to unfamiliar towns or cities. Many "commute" a sizeable distance from their homes to their offices, shops and plants. Children go far away to college. Those reared in a city seek a place in the country; country-bred people and those who grow up in a small town want to live and work in a big city. Family farms and estates disappear in real estate "developments," largely due to the tax burden. Hardly anyone today has a tie to or a longing for a "home place."

The greatest attachment to a home is most often to that which was occupied for several years directly preceding retirement. Upon retirement, the obstacles to moving from it loom large and the will to do so is weak.

The drawbacks to remaining after retirement in the home you occupied just prior to retiring are: an expense geared to a higher income than you will now have; association with a routine you will (necessarily) abandon; an invitation to look to the past.

It is most desirable and beneficial upon retiring to make a complete change in your home, as it is in your lifestyle. It is well to cut the old ties, to move to a new location at some distance from the home in which you retired, to indulge in the stimulation of a fresh start. This suggestion is prompted by two primary considerations: 1) To assure a forward look through a new challenge; 2) To reduce substantially the expense of housing.

136

If you can summon the courage to face a move and overcome the inertia to avoid it, you will be most happy with the result and find the new adventure very stimulating.

However, a word of caution is necessary about buying a "farm" and living the life of a country gentleman.

The advertisements, the scene, the tax advantages, the investment, the lifestyle will appear most attractive. And they are. On the other hand, there are many hazards. Life on a farm depends heavily on competent and reliable help and experienced management.

Most who purchase a farm have had no experience in operating one, have read and studied nothing about this specialized management skill, and are unfamiliar with or refuse to recognize the hazards involved until they own the farm. Nor do they realize the great difficulty in obtaining and keeping necessary, competent, and reliable help.

Experience in several rural areas catering to purchases of farms by retiring city dwellers indicates that the purchases are "turned over" about every seven years due to disillusion and/or frustration.

14 *Appearance*

In retirement, there is a strong tendency (mentioned repeatedly in preceding chapters) to loaf, to take it easy, and with it to be casual and a little careless. Being casual is generally expressed also in dress and other items of personal appearance.

These remarks will apply, in large measure, to men rather than to women.

The retiree fails to shave regularly, gets his hair trimmed less often, disregards the length and cleanliness of his fingernails and wears old, ill-fitting, out-of-style, tattered, and often dirty clothes. Women, to a lesser extent though, wear hair curlers, no makeup, wear "old," not too clean, ill fitting, and unattractive dresses or pants. All of this is supposed to add up to being "comfortable." Perhaps it does.

But being comfortable includes a degree of self-respect and the esteem of others. Dressing well and appropriately, being well groomed, standing straight and looking up—in short, a good appearance—provides a certain pleasure and, surely, satisfaction and confidence. A good appearance requires some effort, and there is less incentive than when you were younger, but not much. And the reward is greater and well worth the effort.

In an informal atmosphere at home one would not want, or be expected, to dress as one would in an office or at a cocktail, lunch, or dinner party. In an informal situation you can, however, shave, brush your hair, bathe, wear clean tieless and coatless leisure clothes that are attractive, appropriate, colorful, clean, and fit well. It is more fun that way. And since you don't *have* to make the effort, it is a more rewarding one. In addition, your friends and admirers won't think that you are letting down, getting careless about your appearance.

I recall an occasion where a man, concerned about his appearance and propriety, was greeted at the dinner table with "Why don't you take off your coat and be comfortable?"

He replied, with a gracious smile, "I will be glad to, if it will make *you* more comfortable; but, frankly, *I'm* more comfortable wearing my coat."

Looking well is therapeutic. It causes you to feel good; it gives you assurance and confidence, a positive attitude. Looking well, you are aware of others noticing you with approval and favor. Altogether, looking well is as important to your well being in retirement as it was before you retired.

And what is looking well? It is several things: being well groomed, well dressed, being alert, attentive, smiling frequently, looking up, standing straight, having a sparkle in your eye, a spring in your step. Some of all of these things present a good image. None of them is difficult to achieve. But, like everything else, as you grow older the achievement requires special attention and much concentration and persistence. Again, however, the effort is well worth the return in satisfaction, in uplift, in living longer and more pleasantly than if you do not make the effort.

Well groomed means, simply, being shaved (every day) or keeping your beard, sideburns, and mustache trimmed; having your hair (as much as there is of it) combed and trimmed to suit your particular style and type in a fashion neither too bygone nor too new; having trimmed and clean fingernails; having clean teeth and inoffensive breath. Obvious and easy? It should be both. But unhappily, it is not!

Most men, and some women, when a special situation does not require it, neglect the niceties of grooming. In contrast, the best soldiers (privates to general officers) in the jungles of the Pacific theater, shaved every morning with cold water in their metal helmets. This extra and unnecessary effort to look sharp made them proud and confident, knowing that they were paying attention to an important detail of looking as soldierly as they could under adverse conditions.

With respect to clothes. When they do not have to go to an office, retired or not, and when they have no social engagement, most men (in addition to not shaving) wear old, discarded, and often tattered and dirty clothes. I am not suggesting that at home and working in the garden you should not be comfortable and relax your usual habit of dress. Quite the contrary. But one can be comfortable dressed in appropriate, colorful, clean, and attractive leisure clothes. And it's more fun that way—you feel better. In this connection, standard and long standing procedure is to advise a man in trouble, especially one overwhelmed by monetary debt, to purchase and wear a new suit! This to build his confidence and self-respect.

You do not need many clothes to appear always to be wearing something different. A suit and an odd pair of slacks and a separate jacket (sports coat) will provide four different combinations. This, it is recognized, is a somewhat easier task for men than it is for women.

A good figure (weight control) is a positive appearance asset, perhaps a necessity. A good figure, we know, depends to a large extent on a balanced and appropriate (for you) diet, exercise, and good posture. These subjects are covered in preceding chapters. It may be well at this point to reread them.

As one grows older, his and her face tends to show it. The marks are largely lines, wrinkles, and a double chin. The cause, however, is not only age itself (failing elasticity and muscle tone and dryness) but often too much sun and failure to exercise and develop the facial muscles.

Your face can maintain a measure of its earlier attraction and freshness and, at least, show only character-denoting lines and very few, if any wrinkles, if you will give your face careful attention before the marks of aging appear.

Some of the things you can do to keep your facial skin healthy and reasonably smooth are these:

Avoid the direct rays of the sun; don't lie on the beach, smothered in "suntan" oil, and bake it. Wear a hat with a large visor or brim when you are working or playing in the sun.

Use daily a "moisturizing" cream (your druggist will have many varieties), which will protect against loss of fluid from the skin and provide increased circulation and improved muscle tone through massage in applying the cream or lotion.

Keep your facial skin clean and unclog the pores by washing with a warm face cloth and then patting your face with cold water.

Visit your doctor to identify and remove incipient skin cancers, unsightly spots, moles, warts, and other such blemishes.

Avoid a "face lift" operation. The contrast is noticeable and, in time, you will need another.

To avoid a "double chin," exercise the muscles between the chin and the throat. One way to do this is to stretch your chin as far forward as you can and massage between your neck and chin with the index finger of each hand. Now open wide your mouth and close it several times by saying "Wa" (open) "hoo" (close); "Wa-hoo," "Wa-hoo"————. Repeat this exercise ten times and do it at least twice a day; better, four times.

The hair on your head and face materially affects your appearance. A full head of hair, even if it is thin, is attractive and you appear to be younger than if you had little hair or are bald. On the other hand, most bald headed men consider the condition a mark of distinction and boast that it indicates superior masculinity. And a mustache or a beard or both cause you to look older than you are. (Which is how some younger men want to look).

Hair styling, if you have enough of it to style, is an important factor in your appearance. An older person, generally, looks a little foolish when his (or her) hair is "done" in a prevailing youthful fashion. A friend of mine aged fifty, let his hair grow long in the current fashion; from the front, one could become used to his somewhat out of character coiffure, but from behind a huge bald spot was evident. That hair-do detracted considerably from his otherwise good appearance.

Surely, a hair styling (cutting) consistent with other physical characteristics, your age and the condition and amount of hair on your head, would add to an attractive impression.

Mustaches, and beards and sideburns should be clean, well-shaped, neat and in accord with one's overall appearance.

The condition and appearance of your teeth surely add to or detract from your total appearance. The role of the teeth with regard to health is included in the chapter "Keeping Physically Fit."

Bright, clean, well-matched teeth are basic to good appearance whether the teeth are natural or dentures. So, in addition to contributing to your good health, care of your teeth and regular visits to the dentist will add to your personal attraction.

A good figure leads one into consideration of good posture as a major element of good appearance. Good posture is standing and sitting straight and taking the time to do the exercises which strengthen the muscles which help you stand and sit straight. Doing so causes you to feel as well as to look good. Good posture is covered in the preceding chapter on health.

Looking up as opposed to looking down at your feet, the floor, or the ground is another factor contributing to an attractive apearance. The habit is relatively easy to acquire. Looking up and ahead reflects a good happy attitude. As in the development of all good habits, looking up requires concentration and constant practice. And the greater and longer the application of these two efforts, the less they are required to achieve the goal. Looking up and ahead contemplates also when talking with others, looking him or her squarely in the eye.

Being interested and showing it is a most desirable personality trait and therefore also an appearance trait. That there is no one so much appreciated as a good listener has been well known for some time. The older and more experienced one is, the more tolerant he or she should be. And, as one interested in new ideas, the better he can listen and try to understand. Then, after listening carefully, the experienced listener may well make a timely, helpul, and even wise comment.

Being retired from time-consuming and exacting routine and conformity you now have the opportunity more fully to express your special individuality, so why not take a little time to do so through your appearance? Why not continue to look the important part you still elect to play?

Surely, you will not want to present the image of being a freak, "way out," or a "hippie," or a man (or woman) on the way down and out. Nor, in all likelihood, will you want to appear to be a fop or a dandy. Would it not be satisfying, even pleasing, on the other hand to be known as a man who dresses well, whose clothes, in town and in the country, on the golf course and tennis court, as a spectator at sporting events, at a cocktail party and at a formal dinner, are appropriate, clean, pressed, colorful, and well put together?

Distinction in the way you dress provides you with an interest and elicits attention and respect from others. At an older age, it would seem inappropriate and will be expensive to adhere to changing fashions. Nor would you want to dress the way you did thirty or forty years ago, if at that time the fashion was markedly different from what it is now.

Fashions for men have not changed much in the last fifty years. Ties are wider or narrower, coat lapels likewise tend to vary between wide and narrow; suits come with vests or without them, in predictable cycles; the collars of shirts have longer or shorter points, are rounded or straight, are tabbed or tabless; trousers (more often called pants) flare or do not and vary with the times between eight and eleven inches wide in the leg. And overall dress tends to be casual or formal. It is easy to be in style by putting aside the clothes you have when you purchase the new styles and using them again when the style reverts to former years, and storing the now outmoded "new" style.

Keeping the foregoing in mind, you can gain a measure of distinction without being "way out" or an anachronism, by setting your own style between the two.

With only a little care on your part, you can be known for (associated with) wearing regimental/striped ties (or small figured ones), silk handkerchiefs that match your ties and socks, for wearing blue, yellow, and pink shirts with long sleeves and the collar fastened by a gold pin, distinctive belts, conservative and well fitting suits, for always having your shoes polished, for wearing an English cap, and for other such items of distinctive and admirable dress.

I recall a well-dressed friend who habitually wore regimental striped neckties. For a Christmas present he received a beautiful, heavy silk, figured necktie manufactured by a prestigious firm. He admired it, but could not bring himself to wear it since it was obviously not his style. He placed it in a drawer with other expensive unwearables.

Sometime later, looking through that drawer, he decided that perhaps he might wear it, just once, "for the hell of it."

That day, a number of people who knew him well remarked, "That's a nice tie, but it isn't the kind you wear!"

Among other qualities, I suppose that one is also typed by the clothes one wears and perhaps that's a good thing. It's one measure of distinction.

As a broad guide to sound and lasting good taste in dress for men, the following may prove both interesting, helpful, and, in some instances, reassuring. It is from an interview with Luciano Franzoni, a noted stylist and clothing consultant, as reported by United Press International. His comments concern the all-time classics in men's wear, based on the demand for them among well-dressed men and their ability to blend them with the style of the moment.

"I don't think people want to get back into the old uniform kind of lifestyle, but they do want to know what they can buy with confidence. They fear being gypped by fads in fashion they can't detect."

A man interested in his clothes needs to consider them in terms of "business" and sports clothes (odd jackets and trousers) for winter and summer if he lives in a seasonal area, and shirts, sweaters, ties and shoes to be worn with each. And then, generally, you will need a dinner jacket and the shoes and accessories that go with it. A blazer with a club or military emblem would also be an item to be considered.

Style is an important factor in all items of dress, particularly in suits, jackets, trousers and vests. For the retiree the old adage of not being the last to discard the old nor the first to embrace the new would seem good advice.

Women confront dress situations broadly similar to men except that there are greater variations and subtleties (and some basics such as a pants suit versus a dress or skirt suit.)

A woman can express distinction in dress through wearing a type of hat, dress, and shoe that emphasizes the best in her height, figure, and color—varying these enough to be in tune with current fashions. In general older women do not look as well in pants as they do in dresses—especially if they are on the plump side.

Maintaining a good appearance is indeed an important element of continuing an active and vigorous life.

15   Coping with Change

A common and persistent human ambivalence is that change is inevitable, but very few welcome change. (Initially, about 90 percent do not.)

It is natural to resist, distrust, and be afraid of change, except those relatively few way-out liberals who want change only for the sake of change. The large majority of us have established routines, customs, ways of doing things, procedures, likes and dislikes, prides and prejudices, to which we have become accustomed, with which we feel at home. We are "comfortable" with certain things, certain people, certain ways. We are used to them. We understand them. We know what to expect and what not to expect. We know our way around. Why change? Why rock the boat—and for what?

But change is inevitable. In one way or another it affects us throughout our lives. There are changes in our neighborhoods, in the type of people moving into them, in their density, in the percentage of children, in the value of the property, in the type of new houses. The type and style of clothes we wear change all too rapidly as does the way women and men wear their hair and the presence or absence of beards and mustaches on men's faces. The morals, habits, behavior, and values of our children and younger adults have changed from those generally respected in our childhoods. And during each of our lives, from childhood to death, we change continually. Change is indeed normal, as well as inevitable.

Local shops are replaced by huge supermarkets with a greater variety of goods at lower prices and with largely self-service and

146

only routine personal contact; country lanes are blacktopped; new interstate throughways slice across scenic and productive farmland; little foreign-made "bugs" of motor cars replace the substantial, roomy, gas-guzzling, American-made family sedan; a new kind of arithmetic is introduced and is found wanting, and college freshmen have to learn to read; schools teach a lot of things we seem to have done well without and fail to provide a reliable ability in the basic "three R's."

We find that interstate motor buses and airplanes have replaced the railroad train in moving us from place to place; that the government provides a lot of things and services we used to feel pride in providing for ourselves; that a small business, because of complicated and confusing regulations and near unbearable taxes, can hardly survive; that radio and television are forming our opinions much more often and effectively than newspapers did (and do); and that people listen and watch a lot, but almost never discuss, and think very little of what they have taken in.

We experience a notable change in formality, in respect for merit and achievement, in the pursuit of excellence, the maintenance of high standards, patriotism, and loyalty, and in the forms of worship. We find the formerly disadvantaged among us treated fairly and given equal opportunity to approaching a reversal of their former status. We notice a growing disrespect for the law and regulations, and disrespect for the will of the majority; lack of integrity and breaches of trust in high places; a tendency to derogate our heroes.

We have, in a relatively short time, materially revised our eating and exercise habits, moved toward a change to the metric system of measurement, and are rapidly gaining in knowledge of our universe.

Change has indeed always been with us. Currently, it is proceeding more rapidly than ever; it is difficult to keep up with it, to understand it fully, and therefore to absorb and go along with it, even eliminating the natural inertia not to.

Change is, of course, frequently cyclical. This is especially true with regard to fashion, custom, values, and other such elements. Feminine, dainty, and elegant attire for women is replaced by the "tweedy, outdoor look," pants suits and dirty torn blue jeans; and then a reverse trend starts. Men's suits have and then do not have vests; trousers are wide, then narrow, then wide again, and so with the width of lapels, ties and shirt collars. Formality gives way to informality which, in turn, is replaced by a return to formality. The almost universal aim of college graduates to become a corporation president gives way to a disdain of business success and doing one's own thing, and then the values change back again.

Always we should recall that twenty years from now, *today* will be "the good old days." And we might reflect that despite the appearance of great change, there is really very little difference in lifestyle, enjoyment, self-expression, and freedom between a feudal serf and a member of one of today's strong labor unions.

Another thought on and observation of change: principles, characteristic actions, situations, and such often remain surprisingly constant. Only their application changes.

One such, for example, is the time a man takes to travel from his home to his place of work, more often than not, his office. Over, say, the last hundred years, the mode of transportation has varied notably, but the time consumed has remained constant at an hour or less.

In New York City in the early days, men walked from their homes below Canal Street (the then canal) to their shops, plants or offices at the lower tip of the island. Later the residential section moved further north and businessmen engaged in financial, wholesale, manufacturing, commercial, and shipping enterprises travelled downtown by carriage, and sometimes on horseback, and then in horse-drawn trams. Then came electric trolley streetcars, then the elevated railway to carry the further uptown residents to their downtown jobs.

Then the wealthier moved to the "country" in the Bronx, then Bronxville, Pelham, and finally up to Rye and the nearby Connecticut shore towns of Greenwich, Stamford, New Canaan, Darien, Westport. The New Haven and Hartford Railroad or the New York Central (serving those inland northerners living in White Plains and northward) carried them to work in New York

City. If they needed to go further up or down town, they rode the subway. A number drove themselves to the City in comfortable automobiles on excellent ''parkways.'' And a large portion of the working population on Manhattan Island traveled to their homes in New Jersey and Staten Island by ferry, tube (under the Hudson River), bridge, and railroad train or bus, and their private automobiles.

But, throughout the years and the changing modes of travel, the ''not in excess of an hour from home to work'' principle held fast.

We might reflect, too, that throughout the ages, things are seldom better or worse than what they were, they are only different!

Those who retire face immediately three dramatic and sudden changes, with widely varying degrees of preparation. These are:

(1) They no longer have a job, or, more properly perhaps, they no longer *have* to go to work to earn an income. They have earned a pension and receive social security payments from the Federal Treasury.

(2) They have eight or more hours free time five days a week (or more) to do with what they will.

(3) Their incomes, in general, are reduced and are less than they were the day before.

Other changes which especially affect the retiree, in addition to those common to all of us, are changes in:

Where he or she (or they) live. And also in the type of house or apartment, the kind of neighborhood, the nature of the climate. The retiree frequently encounters a number of changes in living arrangements even when he does not change the location of his home because of changes in the neighborhood.

Friends and acquaintances. Even if the recently retired person continues to live in the same house he occupied before retirement, there surely will be changes in the people he considers his friends and in his acquaintances. Necessarily, he will see less and less of his former business associates, and people he likes and has not had the time or opportunity to see often will become more frequent companions. And since the retiree will, no doubt, spend more time at places which he seldom frequented when actively employed and less time at some he used to frequent regularly, he will routinely, and unconsciously perhaps, rearrange priorities among his acquaintances.

Keeping in good health. The squash and handball courts and the massage salon are not apt now to be readily accessible. On the other hand, there is more time for exercise and a greater choice of time of day to do it. This requires decision, planning and follow-through.

And now, with the time to enjoy good meals at more liberal and flexible hours and more time for more cocktail parties, decisions and discipline are required to avoid overweight in the new life-style.

The financial situation—requirements, objectives and considerations. These changes may involve investment, insurance, saving, buying, and spending. They will no doubt result in changes in thinking, planning, and action with respect to these areas.

Family relations. The retiree may move to a location closer to some absent members of his family, usually married or working away from home. But, regardless of whether the retired person moves or remains in his preretirement location, the opportunity to visit with children and become better acquainted with grandchildren in their homes or his is increased considerably, wherever they are.

Travel. On the job (before retirement) the retired person in many cases traveled a great deal in the interest of his business. While this may have been (in part and to some extent) fun, it could, as a whole, hardly have been described as pleasurable or relaxed. During vacations while actively employed he may have taken a number of pleasure cruises or motor trips primarily for relaxation and pleasure. Now, however, in retirement, nearly all travel can be, and almost always is, for pleasure and relaxation. This is a considerable change and requires a different approach.

Recreation. We have said several times that there is no such thing as a permanent vacation. A vacation, recreation, has to be related to some otherwise full-time activity, something which you can vacate temporarily, something to which you devote much concentration and so much time that you need now and again to be ''recreated.''

Since, in retirement, the retiree has no full-time responsibility from which to receive relief, recreation takes on a different meaning. It is not, as previously, related to anything. Here, again, a new approach to a changed situation is needed, unless, of course, you find new employment.

Dress. The retired person may in no way change his style of dress. Whether or not he or she does, the *requirement* of dress is relaxed by reason of not reporting daily for work at an office, shop, or plant with its actual or implied prescription of appropriate (and frequently mandatory) attire. So, chances are good that there will be a change. The retiree will doubtless more often wear a ''leisure suit,'' work clothes, sportswear, old and worn clothes. In view of this, he (and she) will need fewer new clothes. Another changed situation with which to reckon.

Community and church activity. In retirement there is a generous amount of time available for volunteer community, church, civic and political service, as a new project or to take an increased responsibility. Communities need capable volunteers at all times. However, they find it difficult to get commitments from busy working people. Thus they welcome, and to a large extent need to rely on, retired people. The availability of so important a resource is certainly a change for the better from the community's viewpoint. And for the retired person, the opportunity and the time to make his or her talents available to the community offers a new challenge and a new satisfaction.

So, in view of all of the changes confronting you in retirement, what do you do? How do you cope with the several substantially changed situations?

Before considering how, you need first, and quickly, to realize that you must and have to, adapt to the changes. This is not always easy. It depends on the extent to which you have prepared for them and on your temperament, and on your lifelong ability to cope with change and other problems. With good sense and determination neither is it difficult.

Now to the "how." Adopting the following attitudes and actions may help in coping successfully with the changes inherent in retirement.

(1) Remember that the marked and dramatic change to "retirement" was, nevertheless, inevitable and expected, even if you were not fully prepared for it. And bear in mind that there is nothing you can do about it. It's done, it's a fact. So now *accept* it and decide to make the most of it.

(2) Consider your retirement a reward, an opportunity, and a challenge: An opportunity to do what you want, with a comparatively great deal of time in which to do it; a challenge to make the best use of that precious, and hard to come by hard-earned, time.

(3) Concentrate on your *new* opportunity, on plans and expected results, on today and tomorrow and the weeks, months and years ahead, on a new lifestyle, new friends, different activities, further accomplishment, with enthusiasm and vigor.

(4) Sharpen your new plans and objectives by discussing them with your family, your friends, and some acquaintances.

In conclusion, and with a little repetition, coping with change, accepting it as normal and inevitable, can be and should be an adventurous, exciting, meaningful and, especially, a very rewarding experience. And, bear in mind that there is no satisfactory alternative!

16   *Faith*

Faith has been a powerful (perhaps the most powerful) influence on the progress of mankind throughout the ages. Faith has inspired men and women to attempt the seemingly impossible and to achieve what were considered unreachable objectives. Faith plays a large part in one's day-to-day life. We have faith in the Lord, in some of our fellow humans, in the stars and the moon and the sun, in our good luck, and too infrequently, in ourselves. And often, unhappily, we think, plan, and act more on faith than on experience and scientifically established fact. Unhappily, faith is often only hope.

Faith has as its companions courage, determination, loyalty, hope and trust.

In our later years we face new problems and different values, with somewhat less enthusiasm and vigor than when we were young. On the other hand we have gained experience, tolerance, patience, and some ability to make sound judgments. To complement and fortify this balanced situation, we need now to strengthen and deepen our faith in God, in nature, in mankind, and in ourselves, and to make it more meaningful. We need faith that if we make a sufficient effort, our objective will be achieved and trouble avoided.

We may well use and stand by the ancient prayer ''Oh God in heaven, I pray thee give me the serenity to accept the things I cannot change, the courage to change those things I can, and the wisdom to know the difference.''

It should be evident that there must be guidance and concern from beyond and above since there is so much evidence of this:

the last minute rescue of all aboard a sinking ship; the miraculous safe landing of an aircraft when one of its two engines fails and its landing wheels are inoperative; the derailment of a train at high speed without a fatality; the bullet aimed at a soldier which is deflected by the stout branch of a tree; the skidding automobile which, by a hair, avoids a crash; the escape from a dungeon; survival of the victim of a maniacal "kidnapper"; the one house in the path of a tornado which is spared its ravages; the unexpected, timely help which avoids financial disaster.

At a time of life which has permitted the development of a measure of wisdom, it may be well to develop also a sort of practical fatalism; a combination of sorts of faith and self-reliance. That is, in any situation, to do all of which one is capable to accomplish or avoid something and then to proceed, or rest, with confidence that it is now in the hands of the Lord. Or, putting this thought another way, it is all right to believe that what will be, will be, provided you are sure that you have taken all reasonable steps to accomplish it and to avoid failure.

A simple illustration: During World War II one night in a remote outpost on New Guinea, three American officers were temporarily secure in a small house while Japanese airplanes were dropping bombs in the area with hardly token resistance. After checking trip wires and the location of small arms, two of the three lay down fully clothed on their cots. The third covered himself with a mosquito net, put an atabrine tablet in his mouth and washed it down with a gulp from his canteen.

"Well, I'll be damned," commented one of his companions, "you may not be *alive* in the morning and you're protecting yourself against *malaria*! Are you nuts? Anyway, if you're going to get malaria, you'll get it."

"No, I'm not nuts and I agree that if I'm going to get malaria, I'll get it, but *I don't want it to be my fault*! So I'm doing all *I* know to avoid getting it. From here on it's in the laps of the gods."

A rereading of the Bible as well as summaries of the thinking of the great philosophers, Plato, Aristotle, Schopenhauer, Bergson, and Dewey will strengthen one's faith in the influences on one's life from beyond and above it and develop an abiding faith in oneself to cope successfully with the world and its people as it really is.

17 Wrap-Up

When you retire, you have some good years ahead. How many depends to a degree on your genetic inheritance, to some extent on luck, and largely on what you do.

If, in the remaining years, you want to loaf, take it easy, "enjoy yourself," leaving your vigorous, active life behind, well and good. Since that is what you want to do, you will enjoy it. And you will gradually rust out, probably in a relatively short time.

If, on the other hand—in tune with nature's and the Lord's design—you continue to be vigorously active pursuing some useful purpose, remain mentally aware and alert, welcome meeting a challenge, and if you value today and constantly look ahead, you will, I submit, enjoy thoroughly the remaining years. You will feel better and enjoy living much more than if you let yourself rust out. Following this route, you will eventually wear out, but it will take some time.

The thoughts developed in this book may be summarized succinctly in these few sentences:

After you are retired, you will enjoy a long, active, and interesting life if you:

(1) Refuse to "retire."
(2) Recognize that you are going either to wear out or rust out, and that it is much more fun and a longer process to *wear out*.
(3) Reflect that hard work never killed anyone, but that worry, lack of purpose, and inactivity have finished many; that the brain and the body need to be actively used to remain healthy.

(4) Consider "retirement" the third, active (but uncommitted) phase of your life, the one in which *you* have full control.
(5) Place emphasis on your current occupation (if only "free lance" or "uncommitted")—what you *are* doing now, not what you *used* to do.
(6) Develop a defined purpose and objectives for your activities, make plans and prepare schedules to implement them.
(7) Accept change as inevitable and as a challenge you can and must meet.
(8) Develop, or continue a *positive* attitude and a *forward* look.

Index